THE
PURE
RELIGION

A BOOK OF THE
NEW MESSAGE
FROM GOD

THE
PURE
RELIGION

AS REVEALED TO
Marshall Vian Summers

THE
PURE
RELIGION

Copyright © 2020 by The Society for the New Message

Edited by Darlene Mitchell
Cover and interior: Designed by Reed Summers

ISBN: 978-1-942293-48-4 (POD)
ISBN: 978-1-942293-49-1 (ebook)
NKL Version 7.05 ; Sv7.4 11/18/19
Library of Congress Control Number: 2019912186

Publisher's Cataloging-in-Publication Data
(Prepared by The Donohue Group, Inc.)

Names: Summers, Marshall Vian, author. | Society for the New Message,
    issuing body.
Title: The pure religion / as revealed to Marshall Vian Summers.
Description: Boulder, CO : New Knowledge Library, the publishing imprint
    of The Society for the New Message, [2019] | Series: The New Message
    from God ; [Volume 1, book 8]
Identifiers: ISBN 9781942293484 (POD) | ISBN 9781942293491 (ebook)
Subjects: LCSH: Society for the New Message--Doctrines. | Religion. |
    Presence of God. | Revelation.
Classification: LCC BP605.S58 S864 2019 (print) | LCC BP605.S58 (ebook)
    | DDC 299/.93--dc23

The Pure Religion is a book of the New Message from God and is published by New
Knowledge Library, the publishing imprint of The Society for the New Message. The
Society is a religious non-profit organization dedicated to presenting and teaching a
New Message for humanity. The books of New Knowledge Library can be ordered at
www.newknowledgelibrary.org, your local bookstore and at many other online retailers.

The New Message is being studied in more than 30 languages in over 90 countries.
The Pure Religion is being translated into the many languages of our world by a
dedicated group of volunteer student translators from around the world. These
translations will all be available online at www.newmessage.org.

The Society for the New Message
P.O. Box 1724   Boulder, CO 80306-1724
(303) 938-8401   (800) 938-3891
011 303 938 84 01 (International)   (303) 938-1214 (fax)
newmessage.org   newknowledgelibrary.org

*W*e shall speak of God, the Higher Authority.

———————

*Th*e Higher Authority is speaking to you now, speaking through the Angelic Presence, speaking to a part of you that is the very center and source of your Being.

———————

*Th*e Higher Authority has a Message for the world, and for each person in the world.

———————

*Th*e Higher Authority is calling to you, calling to you down through the Ancient Corridors of your mind, calling to you beyond your beliefs and your preoccupations.

———————

*F*or God has spoken again and the Word and the Sound are in the world.

From *God Has Spoken Again,*
Chapter 3: The Engagement

THE
PURE
RELIGION

TABLE OF CONTENTS

INTRODUCTION

The Pure Religion is a book of Revelation given by the Creator of all life to the human family through the Messenger Marshall Vian Summers.

Throughout history, God has given Revelation and Wisdom to meet the growing needs of our world at great turning points in the evolution of humanity. Now God is speaking again, delivering a New Revelation to meet the critical needs of humanity as it faces Great Waves of environmental, political and economic change and contact with a Greater Community of intelligent life in the universe.

God's progressive Revelation is continuing anew through a New Message from God, of which *The Pure Religion* is but a part. The words of this text are a direct communication from the Creator of all life, translated into human language by the Angelic Presence that watches over this world, and then spoken through the Messenger Marshall Vian Summers, who has given over 30 years of his life to this process of Revelation.

The New Message from God is an original communication from God to the heart of every person on Earth. It is not for one nation, one tribe or one religion alone. It is a Message for the entire world, a world facing very different needs and challenges from those of ancient times.

This communication is here to ignite the spiritual power of humanity, to sound God's calling for unity amongst the world's nations and religions, and to prepare humanity for a radically changing world and for its destiny in a larger universe of intelligent life.

The New Message from God speaks on nearly every aspect of life facing people today. It is the largest Revelation ever given to humanity, given now to a literate world of global communication and growing global awareness. Never before has there been a

Divine Revelation of this size, given by God to all people of the world at once, in the lifetime of the Messenger.

Yet the New Message from God has not entered the world through the existing religious authorities and institutions of today. It has not come to the leaders of religion or to those who garner fame and recognition. Instead, it has been given to a humble man chosen and sent into the world for this one task, to be a Messenger for this New Message for humanity.

The Messenger has walked a long and difficult road to bring the New Message from God to you and to the world. The process of Revelation began in 1982 and continues to this day. The Messenger's story is one of perseverance, humility and lifelong service to others. His presence in the world today represents an opportunity to know him and receive the Revelation directly from him.

At the center of the New Message is the original Voice of Revelation, which has spoken the words of every book of the New Message. Never before has the Voice of Revelation, the Voice that spoke to the Messengers and prophets of the past, been recorded in its original purity and made available to each person to hear and to experience for themselves. In this way, the Word and the Sound of God's Revelation are in the world.

In this remarkable process of spoken Revelation, the Presence of God communicates beyond words to the Angelic Assembly that oversees the world. The Assembly then translates this communication into human language and speaks all as one through their Messenger, whose voice becomes the vehicle for this greater Voice—the Voice of Revelation.

The words of this Voice have been recorded in audio form, transcribed and are now available in the books of the New Message. In addition, the original audio recordings of the Voice of Revelation are available for all to hear. In this way, the purity of God's original spoken Message is preserved and given to all people in the world.

INTRODUCTION

At this time, the Messenger is engaged in compiling over three decades of spoken Revelation into a final and complete text—The One Book of the New Message from God. This book of Revelation will ultimately be divided into six volumes and possibly more. Each volume will contain two or more books, and each book will be organized by chapter and verse. Therefore, the New Message from God will be structured in the following way: Volume > Book > Chapter > Verse.

The Pure Religion is the eighth book of Volume 1 of the New Message from God and *The Pure Religion* contains 13 individual revelations (chapters) revealed to the Messenger at different times. The Messenger has compiled these revelations into the text you see today.

In order to bring this spoken communication into written form, slight textual and grammatical adjustments were made by the Messenger. This was requested of him by the Angelic Assembly to aid the understanding of the reader and to convey the Message according to the grammatical standards of the written English language.

In some instances, the Messenger has inserted a word not originally spoken in the Revelation. When present, you will often find this inserted word in brackets. Consider these bracketed words as direct clarifications by the Messenger, placed in the text by him alone in order to ensure that ambiguities in the spoken communication do not cause confusion or incorrect interpretations of the text.

In some cases, the Messenger has removed a word to aid the readability of the text. This was usually done in the case of certain conjunctions (words such as *and, but*) that made the text unnecessarily awkward or grammatically incorrect.

The Messenger alone has made these slight changes and only to convey the original spoken communication with the greatest clarity possible. None of the original meaning or intention of the communication has been altered.

The text of this book has been structured by the Messenger into verse. Each verse roughly signals the beginning or ending of a distinct message point communicated by the Source.

The verse structure of the text allows the reader to access the richness of the content and those subtle messages that may otherwise be missed in longer paragraphs of text that convey multiple topics. In this way, each topic and idea communicated by the Source is given its own standing, allowing it to speak from the page directly to the reader. The Messenger has determined that structuring the text in verse is the most efficacious and faithful way of rendering the original spoken revelations of the New Message.

Through this text, we are witnessing the process of preparation and compilation being undertaken by the Messenger, in his own time, by his own hands. This stands in stark contrast to the fact that the former great traditions were rarely put into written form by their Messengers, leaving the original messages vulnerable to alteration and corruption over time.

Here the Messenger seals in purity the texts of God's New Message and gives them to you, to the world and to all people in the future. Whether this book is opened today or 500 years from now, God's original communication will speak from these pages with the same intimacy, purity and power as it did the day it was first spoken.

Though it appears to be a book in the hand, *The Pure Religion* is something far greater. It is a calling and a communication from the Heart of God to you. In the pages of this book, God's Presence calls to you and to all people, calling for you to awaken from the dream and nightmare of living in Separation apart from your Source, calling to the presence of "Knowledge," the deeper spiritual Intelligence that lives within you, waiting to be discovered.

INTRODUCTION

The Pure Religion is part of a living communication from God to humanity. Remarkably, you have found the New Message from God, or it has found you. It is no coincidence that this is the case. This opens the next chapter in the mystery of your life and of your presence in the world at this time. The door opens before you. You need only enter to begin.

As you enter more deeply into the Revelation, the impact on your life will grow, bringing a greater experience of clarity, inner certainty and true direction to your life. In time, your questions will be answered as you find growing freedom from self-doubt, inner conflict and the restraints of the past. Here the Creator of all life is speaking to you directly, revealing to you the greater life that you were always destined to live.

The Society for the New Message from God

THE PURE RELIGION

As revealed to
Marshall Vian Summers
on March 23, 2013
in Boulder, Colorado

It is a great misfortune that people have been so discouraged by the state of religion and the history of religion in this world—all of the violence that it has produced, corruption, misunderstanding and confusion. It is a demonstration of what people do with God's Revelations when they are not guided by the power of Knowledge within themselves. Here religion becomes a tool of the state, a resource for ambitious people, another distinction that one tribe will use to overwhelm or overcome another.

Of course, this has driven people away and has traumatized people, even in current times, to the point where God's New Revelation must be given in a pure form, notwithstanding the great value, depth and wisdom of God's earlier Revelations and their importance in building human civilization in the world.

But God must speak again, for the Message must be clarified. The purpose of religion must be clarified. And the meaning and purpose of your life must be elevated and clarified. Otherwise, religion becomes a great problem in the world, whereas it was meant to be a great solution at the outset.

If you look at this without condemnation, you will see the great need for Knowledge [the deeper spiritual Mind] within yourself. For without Knowledge, you will misuse everything. You will misuse nature; you will misuse your mind; you will misuse your body because you are operating from a position of confusion. Uncertain who you are, why you are here and what you are doing, you will be governed by foreign powers and outside influences. Such is the tragedy of living in Separation [from your Source], a tragedy that exists throughout the universe.

So a great clarification must be given for religion and every aspect of religion—a great clarification about God; a great clarification about redemption and what that means and how it is achieved; a great clarification that unites all the world's religions, for they have a common Source.

What is religion? Why is it necessary? Why is it impossible to extinguish it from the human heart and mind completely? Religion represents the expression of your deeper nature and the need of your deeper nature to have this expression in life, to give voice and form to this, which is so essential and elemental to who you are, where you have come from and what you will be returning to when you leave this world. It is fundamental to your deeper nature and to everything you really are—everything that can be seen and not seen, both the manifestation and the mystery of your life.

Religion is not an ideology. Religion is not a building or an organization or a hierarchy of organizations. In essence, it is the movement of God within you and between you and others functioning in the world. For God serves the world, working through people from the inside out.

God does not manage the weather or the geological forces of Earth. God has set all that in motion at the beginning of time. It is all operating on its own. Your challenge is to adapt to it and to utilize it meaningfully and beneficially, for yourself and for others. This, of course, would be impossible if Knowledge had not been given to you—the great endowment to guide you, protect you and prepare you for a greater life.

The fact that Knowledge has been forgotten, or is unknown in this world to such a large extent, creates the dilemma for religion because without Knowledge, religion becomes rules and prescriptions, admonitions, and invariably turns into a form of great oppression for the people. Given at the outset perhaps to help them organize their thinking and their lives, it becomes a yoke to harness them, and the spiritual light goes out of their lives.

This is not God's intention. God's intention is that people will discover the great endowment of Knowledge that the Lord of the universe, the Lord of countless religions and races in the universe, has bestowed upon this world. But when Knowledge is lost, fear and imagination take over. Confusion reigns. People are corralled to work and to live in servitude. Such has been the case throughout the history of the human family.

So God has given now a pure Message and has provided the Steps to Knowledge as its foundation so this will not be merely another belief to compete with existing beliefs, another ideology that must be defended and debated and used to overwhelm or oppress others.

For God has given the Steps to Knowledge not to one race or tribe or group, not to one region alone, but to all the peoples of the world, to be used in all the faith traditions of the world, to be recognized as the key Message of God to God's Creation living in Separation in the physical reality.

So what is religion as an institution or a body of teachings? In essence, its purpose is to create an environment and an encouragement for people to experience the Presence, the Power and the Grace of God within themselves, their lives, within each other and within the world.

What does this mean? This means that the purpose of religion is to bring people to the great endowment, to the endowment of Knowledge, for this is how God will guide you and move you and restrain you—carrying you forward, holding you back, a greater force beyond words or expression. Beyond the realm and the reach of the intellect it is.

This is the pure religion. It has been the religion of the saints, the great creators and humanitarians. Moved by a greater power and force in their lives, beyond the ordinary things that determine people's lives and experiences, they have been moved by a greater force, like a spiritual gravity, moving them to do extraordinary things for the benefit of others, beyond mere kindness and doing favors or service for people, by setting an example and encouraging and igniting the power of Knowledge in others.

You can forget the name of famous generals and leaders of nations, famous politicians, famous artists even, but the names of the great saints will prevail because their contribution has been the greatest and the most lasting and profound. They serve even today, their great gifts resonating continually through the human heart and mind, reminding people that who they are is greater than their minds and their bodies, reminding people that they are part of a Greater Reality, beyond what their senses can report.

This is the pure religion at work, you see, because God redeems you through the power and presence of Knowledge working in your life.

To the degree to which you can recognize it, yield to it and follow it intelligently, this is how God will redeem you.

For Knowledge is not bound by your culture or your beliefs. Knowledge is not bound by tradition. It moves beyond these things. In this way, people can do things that are extraordinary and mysterious, creating value and benefit that is beyond human understanding. They become a demonstration of the great endowment.

Ritual and ideology are valuable, however, in setting a precedent or a pathway. People need this to get started and to use it to help them balance their lives, to give them structure and orientation. It is like preparing to fly, preparing to fly the aircraft. You have to study first. You have to become oriented first. You have to learn about the physics, the environment, the winds and aviation before you can take the helm of the aircraft. This is what ritual and ideology are for, to orient you, to prepare you for flight.

But the experience of flying is a different matter. Here you step beyond the boundaries of intellectual understanding and enter into the Mystery—the Mystery that is pure and uncontaminated by the world, the Mystery that is not governed by magic or romance and the search for power. This is the pure Mystery. This is the pure religion because here you are engaging with God directly in ways that are essential and elemental to you.

You cannot use this power for yourself. It is not there for you to govern or to direct. Indeed, it is there to govern you and to direct you. But it requires your intelligence. It requires your self-awareness. It requires responsibility and restraint and true compassion for others, or it will not emerge.

That is why the ambitious are never chosen. That is why the great Messengers throughout time have been reluctant, accepting reluctantly the great task set before them. While everyone else might want to use religion for power or benefit, the true Messengers are reluctant. They are honest. They are simple. They are prepared for great service.

Beyond ideology and belief and arguing about these things, and the constant and endless debate over these things in the attempt to understand with your mind something that exists beyond the mind's realm and reach, you must enter the pure religion. Whether you are a Christian, a Buddhist, a Jew, a Muslim or of any other tradition, or of no tradition at all, the pathway to God is open to you.

God has spoken again now to give a clear pathway, to give clarity to people of all faiths and nations and to illustrate the central importance of the great endowment, the endowment of Knowledge. For you cannot come to God based upon belief alone. You cannot truly improve your life or the lives of others on belief alone, for not everyone will share these beliefs.

God knows that not all people will follow one teaching or adhere to one teacher, no matter how great they are. God knows this, but people are confused.

This is the antidote to all of the misuse of religion in the world. This is the antidote to human greed, confusion and oppression carried out in the name of religion. Here God is desecrated. God's Will and Purpose are maligned. Here everything that is sacred and profound becomes lost and degraded.

THE PURE RELIGION

You who seek to know your greater purpose in life and the meaning for your being here must have a new experience of the Divine if you are suffering under these results and consequences.

That is why God has spoken again, not to replace the world's religions, but to elevate them and to prepare them for the great change that is coming to the world, and for humanity's encounter with a universe of intelligent life. For none of God's previous Revelations can do this, you see. It is part of a Greater Plan that will always be far beyond human understanding and comprehension.

This is the Mystery. God lives in the Mystery. People live in the manifestation. They try to make the Mystery a manifestation. But the Mystery is always the Mystery.

You must have strength and courage, then, to go beyond the manifestations of religion. You must be very honest. Your motives must be clear, or you will not be able to proceed. The pure religion requires a clarity and a purity of intention if you are to enter there.

Do not demean religious traditions and ceremonies and teachings and practices, for they are for people at the outset. Though they may be misused and misunderstood, they are providing structure at the outset, which can be very helpful for many people. But unfortunately these things become religion itself.

People teach that if you do not believe according to a certain prescription or a teaching from antiquity, you will not be received in Heaven. Yet God presides over a universe of countless races and religions, so clearly it is not belief or ideology that brings you across the threshold into the Divine Presence.

God will not punish you for failing because God knows that without Knowledge, you could only be in confusion and make mistakes, even terrible mistakes.

That is why taking the Steps to Knowledge is so fundamental to what religion really is and what it must be, for God redeems you here—not in your mind, not in your thoughts, not in your beliefs. For if you ever do return to your Ancient Home, which you will eventually, you will find people there with all kinds of beliefs, coming from beliefs that are totally different, coming from other worlds, coming throughout the universe. Can you imagine such a thing? You cannot. You cannot.

But the Mystery is in your life. It is in your heart. You cannot divorce yourself from it entirely. People try. They are very busy all the time. They do not want to sit still for a moment. They do not want to really feel what they feel about their lives, or they will have a crisis. Because the Presence is always there, waiting, calling with a natural attraction.

This is the pure religion. But to even consider this is possible or beneficial, you must have faith in the human heart. If you think people are fundamentally evil and prone to evil, then you will think of religion as a way to harness and corral them, to crack the whip over them and to threaten them with damnation and all manner of torture and misery if they do not follow what you tell them. People think this is how God is.

An all-merciful God is all merciful. An all-knowing God is all knowing. God knows without the power and presence of Knowledge, you cannot lead your life truly. So God gives you the Steps to Knowledge. They were given before in ancient times, but forgotten or dismissed, for those who ruled over religion did not trust the human heart.

But now humanity is literate. It is aware of the greater world it lives in to a certain extent. You are not isolated, primitive tribes anymore. Though your tendencies may still be primitive and self-destructive, you are aware of greater things.

God must prepare you for the world and for life beyond the world and for the degree of unity that will have to happen naturally between people if humanity is to preserve this world as a livable place and preserve its freedom and self-determination in the universe, where freedom is very rare.

It is your deepest needs and the need of the world itself that have brought God's New Revelation to the world. It is the first Revelation of this kind in over 1400 years.

You are living at a time of Revelation. But you must understand the different levels of religion. There is religion to take care of people and feed them. There is religion to organize culture and society basically. There is religious belief, which can help people, to a certain degree. But then there is the pure religion, which brings people into the engagement with Knowledge within themselves and the Greater Powers in the universe that the God of the universe directs for the welfare of all peoples and nations.

When you enter the mystery of this, you have to leave behind your fixed beliefs, your ideology. You have to have the strength and faith and courage to do this, or you will be left outside the inner sanctum of the temple. For belief will not bring you to the God of all life. It will take a greater engagement, a more profound engagement, and a life guided by the great endowment, which lives within you at this moment.

People will argue against this. They say, "Humans cannot be trusted. They are evil. They are corrupted. They have fallen from grace." This is ridiculous. Separation was created because part of Heaven wanted to experience it, and so here you are. It is too great and profound to ever comprehend.

You have left God, but God has not left you. You are lost in your thoughts, your fears, your desires and your preoccupations, but the Presence goes with you. For there is a part of you that has never left God, and this is the part of you that is called Knowledge.

That is why God will redeem you in the end, and everyone else, because you cannot separate yourself from your Source. You can live in Separation. You can live in fantasy. You can live a life of degradation and crime and poverty and self-abuse, but you cannot break the connection.

Someday, eventually, you will turn to the power within—exhausted, frustrated, overwhelmed. You will turn to this power, and it will begin a long process of redemption, putting you in service to others in the simplest and most humble ways so that your value and dignity and self-respect can be restored. For you cannot return to your Ancient Home a miserable, defiled creature. And you are not sent into the world merely to have your life be lost and wasted here.

The mind is an important tool, but it is not the platform for ultimate truth. Belief and ideology can be helpful at the beginning, but a hindrance towards the end. You must step beyond the pavement into the wilderness because God is there. You must learn to be still. You must learn to listen within yourself. You must restrain your passions and your grievances and your admonitions to give yourself this chance.

It is a different way of being in the world. It is a blessed way of being in the world. And though you are confused and do not know what you are doing and things are changing, you have turned a corner. You are beginning the return.

God knows the way to God. People never know the way to God. But you do not need to know the way to God because God knows the way. You need only ask and pray with great determination that the engagement can begin for you, and to take the Steps to Knowledge that God has provided, and to teach you how to listen to the deeper voice within you—not the voice of your culture, your family, your greed or your fear, or the greed or the fear of the world or any force in the world that is unholy, but the true voice. It will be the most natural thing for you to do this.

This is the pure religion. It can be practiced within the mosque, the temple, or the church, or anywhere. It is waiting for you to respond. It is waiting for you to realize your great need for this, for only God can fulfill and direct you in the world. Whether you are religious or not, whether you practice a religion or not, whether you believe in a religion or not, God's Plan will save you if you can respond.

Here there are no religious wars. Here there is no religious oppression. Here all faiths coexist because they are all means to the same end. They are all feeding the deeper yearning of the heart if they are true and authentic.

We bring you now to the pure religion so that you may embrace it and see how important it is and how central to your life and your destiny, your fulfillment and your true self-expression it really is. This is a gift of Heaven for you, a gift that comes from a greater Source—given now in terms you can understand and that can be translated into different languages effectively; given now with the Will and the Intention of Heaven.

You suffer because you do not know why you are sent and who sent you and what you have to do next to begin to reclaim this experience and understanding of your life. Rich or poor, this confusion will haunt you until you seek for true resolution.

This begins the sacred engagement. This begins the sacred return. Here God does not take you away from the world, but brings you into the world in an entirely new way. Here you see the need for Knowledge everywhere around you, and you do not condemn people for their failures and mistakes. Here you become an expression of Heaven as you seek to strengthen Knowledge in others and to serve people in the most fundamental ways, wherever it is necessary for you to do so.

If you have been abused by religion or confused by it, understand these words. See this great opening and opportunity for you. For your relationship with God is the most pivotal relationship in life, and the degree to which you can accept it and experience it and be part of it determines how far you can go in relationship with anyone. If you cannot be intimate with the power that resides within, how can you be really intimate with anyone? How can you be trusting if you cannot trust what is within you? How can you be open and allow your true affection to emerge if you do not have the guidance and power of Knowledge within yourself?

This restores your true relationship with yourself, which fundamentally is your relationship with Knowledge. From this, you begin to have the basis and the foundation for the great relationships you are meant to have in life, which will come to you as you are prepared, as you are freed enough from the past to receive them and to understand their meaning.

Here you begin to live the pure religion in what you say and what you do and even what you think. This is a Power greater than the world and everything in the world—greater than nature, greater than the physical forces that move the world. For now you are finding that part of you that is timeless and changeless, which will give you freedom from death and a sense of your great permanence, even through your journey here on Earth.

CHAPTER 2

THE GREAT FAITH

As revealed to
Marshall Vian Summers
on April 25, 2007
in the Old City, Jerusalem, Israel

It is necessary now to consider what real faith is in the light of great change in the world. With the coming waves of change that will sweep across the face of the world, with the Greater Darkness that is in the world, your understanding of faith must change. It must take a higher ground, a more secure position, a more authentic understanding and expression.

This faith then must be based upon what is unseen, not upon what is seen. It must be based upon what is known and most deeply felt. It cannot be based upon appearances. It cannot be based upon the manifestations of nations or religions, or it will suffer terribly and fail you in the time of crisis and great need.

Your faith must be in something greater than what humanity has created. It must be something greater than what the institutions of the world have created.

You see, your faith is meant to keep your mind focused on a greater power that resides within you and within the minds and hearts of all who dwell here. It is this power within you and around you that must be the focus and the substance of your faith.

For consider, if your faith is based upon the manifestations of life—the creations of humanity, what human institutions have developed—then how can it be sustained into the future? What will happen to your faith when nations clash, when terrible acts are committed against innocent people in the name of God and religion? What will happen to your faith when people go hungry and starvation increases as the world's supply of fresh water and food declines due to environmental degradation and overuse? What will happen to your faith when holy sites are desecrated, when places beloved by people are destroyed through turmoil, through competition, conflict and war?

What will happen to your faith within these scenarios? If you believe that God is the author of all that takes place, how will you justify these things? How will you keep God holy and merciful and beneficial if you think God is the author of human behavior and human conflict?

There must be a clarification here. There must be a greater understanding, or faith will fail you if it has not done so already.

There are many people today whose faith has already been shattered. They have grown cynical, and their fear has become justified. They do not believe in a greater promise for humanity. And if they are religious, they will think that humanity will suffer under the weight of God's recrimination and punishment.

They think these things because they have lost faith in what is most essential in life. They are unaware of the great endowment of Knowledge—a greater Intelligence that has been given to the human family, which resides within each heart as a potential within each person.

They have seen their dreams be shattered through human conflict, corruption and degradation. And now their heart is closed and their minds are dark. They will easily succumb to the Greater Darkness in the world, which can speak to their fear and their anger and their distrust.

They are unaware of the great endowment from the Creator of all life. It is this endowment—this deeper Intelligence, this mysterious power, this invisible force—that must be the source of your faith.

Everything around you can change. Everything around you is subject to destruction and to desecration. But what God has placed within you is beyond the reach of human deception and corruption. It is beyond the reach of manipulation and seduction by any force, whether it be a human force or a force from beyond the world.

This greater power within you is here to guide you and to protect you—to guide you to your greatest expression in life and your greater contributions to the world and to all life here. It is within you at this moment. And it will be within you each moment regardless of what happens on the outside.

If your faith is in things seen and touched, you are placing yourself in great vulnerability. You are assuring that your future will be filled with anger and disappointment, shock and tragedy.

You are entering very turbulent times in the world. The world is in decline. Its resources are diminishing. Yet human populations continue to grow. There has been great damage to the life-sustaining resources of this world. The environment has been compromised to a very serious degree. And there are forces from beyond the world who are here to take advantage of a weak and divided humanity.

Where will your faith stand in the face of all these great travails and challenges? How will you maintain your focus on the great promise for humanity? How will you avoid losing faith in yourself, in other people, in nations, in governments, and in God, as your world undergoes cataclysmic change? Your life then is destined to immense disappointment, confusion and disillusionment if your faith is in things that are seen and heard and touched.

It is the greater power of Knowledge—the Mystery, the evidence of things unseen—that must be the focus of your faith; that must be the heart of your religion; that must be the source of your encouragement, your wisdom and your guidance.

This is the great faith. This is the faith that requires reinforcement. This is the faith that will ask of you to place your confidence in a greater unseen power—a power that you may only experience intermittently, or even rarely.

This power has been known to the true practitioners of religion throughout the ages, but it goes unrecognized for nearly all the people [today] regardless of their nation or their faith tradition.

This is why there is a New Message from God in the world—a Message to restore this faith, to emphasize its importance, to show you how it provides you freedom from vulnerability, freedom from anger, freedom from disappointment and disillusionment.

For you may lose faith in all things seen and touched, but the faith in Knowledge must remain strong. If this can be the case, then you will be able to withstand the Great Waves of change without losing your appreciation for your Divine nature or the Divine nature of others who dwell here. You will be able to practice forgiveness and tolerance and restraint—things that you would lose otherwise without this great faith.

This great faith assures that the Power of God is there to guide you and to protect you and to lead you to great accomplishments in life. Without such a faith, you would not see this greater possibility. You would not recognize the signs within yourself. You would not heed the direction that is provided.

For you would be overtaken by the world around you—swayed by the grievances and the rage and the conflict that you see and hear around you. You would be lost—swept away by the Great Waves of change, overtaken by human suffering, overwhelmed by a world you could not understand. And your mind would become filled with anger, fear and revenge.

Your destiny then becomes clear, for without this greater faith you will fall into darkness. You will lose your connection to Divinity. You will pray for things to change. You will pray for things to get better. You will pray for your life to be spared. But all your prayers will be filled with fear and misunderstanding. They will not be based upon the great faith that you must have if you are to endure the Great Waves of change and to be a light in the world of darkness.

For Knowledge is not simply here to guide and protect you. It is here to enable you to discover and to express the greater gifts that you have brought into the world.

You have come into the world at a time of great change and upheaval. This great change and upheaval—instead of defeating you, instead of sending you into confusion and darkness—will actually call forth from you the gifts that you have come to give. For this is the world that you have come to serve. And its circumstances will give definition to your greater purpose and meaning here.

Perhaps you can begin to see here that the very circumstances that would defeat you otherwise are those circumstances that will illuminate you, that will call forth your greater gifts to the world. This is an entirely different response than the response of most people around you. This is an entirely different response than you would have if the great faith were not sustained within you.

For whether humanity is rising or falling, the power of Knowledge lives within you. And you can amplify this power in others by sharing the great faith with them, by sharing the New Message from God with them, which speaks of this great faith and emphasizes its vital importance both now and in the future.

This is the Power of God within you. This is your connection. This is what will fulfill the deeper need of your soul, which goes unsatisfied by all the pleasures and excitements of the world. For it needs to realize its purpose and to fulfill it here in the world. That is the great need of your soul. And that need can be satisfied even if civilizations are clashing, even if all hope seems to be lost in the minds and hearts of people around you.

Who will guide them, then, except one who has this great faith? Who will restore them and give them strength, courage and wisdom except those who have this great faith? Who will be a light unto the world, and who will be able to counteract the Greater Darkness in the world except those who have this great faith?

Who will be able to see beyond the divisions of religious ideology and historical interpretation, and who will be able to mend the conflicts that exist between the world's religions except those who have this great faith? Who will be the peacekeepers and the peacemakers, who will not turn to violence, who will not take sides and struggle except those with this great faith?

You must have faith, then, in what the Creator of all life has placed within you to guide and to protect you, and to lead you to your greater expression and accomplishment in the world.

Your confidence in anything else must be very reserved and conditional. For so much will change, and you must allow this change to happen. You may speak out against it and you may try to offset its more damaging consequences, but you must allow this change to occur.

What you can give to people is food, water, shelter and the great faith. Taking care of people, feeding people, assisting people and giving them the great faith—that is what will be needed. For it is only the great faith that will give humanity a future. It is only the great faith that will enable you and others to navigate the difficult waters ahead. It will be your raft in the turbulent seas.

Only this great faith will show humanity that it has great cause to unite in its own defense and for the protection of the world. It is this, then, that will allow humanity to have a greater future—a future greater than its past. But this future will not be based upon political mandates or religious ideologies. It will be established and built upon a great faith.

For only the power of Knowledge within you can withstand the vicissitudes of life and the conflicts of the world. It is here on a mission within you and within each person to make a specific and unique contribution to a world in change. Knowledge within you is fully prepared to deal with the difficulties ahead even though you yourself are not.

Only this great Knowledge within you can remain pure and unaffected even though people around you will be enraged and terrified and uncertain. It is certainty, then, born of Knowledge that will be your true counsel and your true guide, and will be the evidence of a Greater Power within you and within the world.

You work for the good. You will try to alleviate suffering. But you must do this under the guidance of Knowledge, or the world will capture you and take you away. You will fall into its divisions and its conflicts. You will take sides, and you will struggle, and you will fight.

Even your desire to serve humanity must be guided by this greater power within you. Otherwise, your desire to give will be built upon your own ambitions, your own ideals, your own grievances. It will not be pure and it will not be effective. Your desire for a better world, and even your ideas to establish a better world in whatever field that you are interested in or in which you have expertise, must also be guided by Knowledge, or your ideas and your actions will not be effective.

For only God has an answer for the future. You do not have an answer. The change that is upon humanity is far too great for your intellect to comprehend. It is far too great for your intellect to solve without this great faith and without this great power.

In a way, you and humanity itself [have been driven] to a point of desperation where you must find the power of Knowledge or risk failure and collapse.

That is why there is a New Message from God in the world because it is only this New Message that can save humanity. It is only this New Message now that can overlook the divisions of humanity—the divisions of culture, the divisions of religion, the divisions of race and economic power. It is only this great faith that is unaffected by the past—by the turbulent, violent and grave history of the human family.

This is the need of the soul: the need to find and fulfill its mission in the world. For you are not here by accident. You have not simply washed upon the shore. You have come for a purpose. You have come to serve a world in need and to make a unique and specific contribution. But only Knowledge within you really knows what this is.

People are very impatient and want to have the answer right away, so they create an answer that is appealing to them, that makes them feel good and comfortable, safe and secure. But these notions, these ideas and these propositions have no power in the face of the Great Waves of change. They will crumble under the weight of human destiny. They are mere wishes. They have no strength, no wisdom, no security to them.

You must have a greater power within you to rely upon. You must have a greater faith in this power. It must not be built upon things that you can see and touch, upon ideas and belief systems, upon systems of belief. It must have a greater foundation. For the foundations of religion and the foundations of government will all be shaken and in some cases will even collapse in the face of the Great Waves of change.

You must have a foundation that is greater than the world. And you must strengthen this foundation by taking the Steps to Knowledge, by learning The Way of Knowledge, by receiving God's New Message and by recognizing this great faith in all the great religious traditions of the world.

For the great faith is not new. It has only been forgotten. It has only been overshadowed by ritual and history and belief. It has been forgotten. People believe in institutions, in sanctuaries, in rituals, in historical interpretations. They follow great leaders, avatars, saviors or saints. But they have forgotten the most important thing. And that is the great faith.

When you pray to the great faith, ask for it to become strong and to guide you—to reveal to you your errors, to show you your weakness, to show you what you must correct, what you must strengthen and what you must set aside. Ask for its counsel and its wisdom, but also ask for the strength to follow it, the courage to follow it and the freedom that it will give you from all other obligations.

If you are to follow the great way, you must have this strength, this courage and this freedom. It does not all happen at once. You acquire it incrementally, step by step. You build your connection to Knowledge. You become aware of Knowledge and sensitive to it. You begin to heed its messages and its warnings. You feel the restraint, and you allow it to propel your life in certain directions.

You learn over time to distinguish the power of Knowledge from all other forces within your mind—from all other compulsions and impulses, ideas and persuasions. This takes time to learn and to develop. You must learn these things and develop these things if the great faith is to become substantial and real to you and if its immense service to you and to humanity is to be realized.

Therefore, recognize what deserves your faith and your devotion. Realize that that which is unseen has all of the power and that which is seen is what is vulnerable and weak. Here you will see that God is great and the world is small, that nations and religions are vulnerable and that human weakness is everywhere.

And you will see that everything that occurs to you in life will either show you the evidence of Knowledge or the need for Knowledge, and that everything that happens will substantiate your great faith, the greater faith that you must now have. For this is your future and this is your promise. This is your calling and this is your mission.

Allow God's New Message to reveal this to you without compromise, without distortion from the past. Then you will be able to see its evidence in all the great religious traditions. And you will see the great teachers and the great Messengers from the past in a different light. And you will understand their actions and their mission far more clearly, for your mission will be emerging within you slowly as you take the Steps to Knowledge.

May the power and the presence of Knowledge be with you this day. May your mind become still. May you learn to listen and to discern the evidence of the greater power within you. May you abide with it and may you give it your great faith, for here your faith finds its true home and its true expression.

CHAPTER 3

THE SACRED

As revealed to
Marshall Vian Summers
on April 29, 2008
in Esfahan, Iran

It is time now to speak of the Sacred—what is truly sacred, what must be revered, what must be recognized—and to see how it is very different from the things that are considered sacred and held to be sacred by many people.

For what is sacred cannot be touched. It cannot be named. It cannot be held within your hands. It is not a place. It is not a building. It is not an object. For what is sacred is what is permanent.

For in the beginning, there was the Sacred. In the end, there was the Sacred. In the middle, in between, there was the Sacred. It is past. It is present. It is future. It is a moment of experience. It is a revelation.

It is a memory stretching back through the corridors of your mind, so far back that it reaches beyond this life, beyond this set of circumstances. It is like remembering something that has always been, but has been forgotten.

When people have this experience, they know there is something permanent in their lives. It is not a belief that something is permanent. It is not a belief based upon fear and apprehension. It is not an accommodation to offset the anxiety that accompanies the awareness of one's mortality and limited life here in the world. The Sacred is like a flame that never burns out.

When people have a sacred experience, or when someone in the past in history has had a sacred experience, people hold certain places to be sacred where events occurred, where sacrifices were made. These places are held to be sacred, and beautiful monuments are created—some of them so beautiful that people come from everywhere to visit them, to pay homage, to experience them.

But they are not sacred. If you knew what was really sacred, you would understand this. If you have experienced what is sacred, you would understand this. There would be no issue here. You would not argue.

In some traditions, the Earth itself is considered sacred—the entire Earth, not just one particular place. But the Earth is not sacred. It is just the Earth.

This building—however beautiful, however historical, however ornate or phenomenal—is just a building. This statue or this object, it is just a statue or an object. To make it sacred, to insist or believe it is sacred is to miss the point. For it might be sacred to you or to your culture, but it is not sacred to others. To them, it is interesting or beautiful. It is just a thing, however. It is not sacred to them.

But anyone who has the experience of the Presence of God or the movement of Knowledge within themselves will know it is sacred. So different it is from anything else—from any idea, from any belief, from any place, from any tradition or ritual—that to anyone who experiences it, it will be sacred or, at the very least, remarkable and confounding.

THE SACRED

To know the Sacred is to be relieved of so much confusion and so much hostility and so much attachment to things. For God is not attached to these things. And the greater Intelligence that God has placed within you—the deeper Mind, the Mind of Knowledge—it is not attached to these things either.

But the mind—the mind of the world, the mind that you think with—it makes things sacred. It has its own gods. Unaware of the great Presence, unaware of the Fire of Knowledge burning within you, it creates its own sacred events, sacred places, sacred people, sacred objects and so forth.

It is okay to honor a place where something sacred has occurred, or to honor a person who demonstrated what is sacred in their life in the most authentic way. But do not call these places sacred, for that is confusion. Pass through these places, honor or remember the person or the event, but hold what is sacred for what *is* sacred.

For what is sacred is not an object. It is not a book. It is not a place. It is not even an event. These are all things in time through which the Sacred moves.

If you can know what is sacred, you can experience it anywhere. It will be with you anywhere. It can speak to you anywhere. It can move you, the deeper movement of your life, anywhere.

Passions may come and go. Great romances may come and go. Life experiences may come and go. You may experience great beauty or great tragedy, creation and destruction, dramatic events and mundane events—but what is Sacred remains there.

It is still, and it is moving. It is so still that you have to become still to experience it. Yet it is moving—because you were sent here to do something, to give something, to recognize something and to unite with certain people for a greater purpose. This is sacred, too, this movement.

It is not like God is some distant star. God is moving in your life— moving through the world, moving through people, places and events because everyone was sent here to give something, to do something. And the fact that people have not experienced this—or recognized this or fulfilled this—is the root of everyone's suffering.

Yet many people know there is something sacred in life, so they try to give some expression of this—the sacred cow, the sacred temple, the sacred book, the sacred history, the sacred object, the sacred Sun, the sacred Earth—even the heavens, the universe, the Greater Community.

Yet what is Sacred moves through all these things, moves like the wind. You cannot capture it. You cannot hold onto it. You cannot show it to another and say, "This is it. Believe in this."

Sacred objects become lost. Great temples are destroyed or fall away. Even the sacred Earth in the far distant future will no longer be here, and everything that was considered sacred upon it will no longer be here.

But the Sacred remains. It is in the Mystery. You must have the courage and the confidence to enter the Mystery, to be still.

People cannot be still because they are afraid—afraid of what they might feel, what they might know, what they might see. For these things are already within them, waiting to be discovered. People are afraid of themselves. They are afraid of life. They are afraid of change. They are afraid of God. Yet all these things exist within them, waiting to be discovered.

For those who have experienced the Mystery, for those who have experienced the Sacred, it is more real than anything you can touch, anything you can think, anything you can see or hear or hold in your hands. They become less real, less significant.

You are free now to pass through life like the wind, like the Presence, like the Sacred. Yes, you are still a person, and you have obligations and difficulties. You have pains and you suffer for things. There are disappointments. There is frustration. But there is something Sacred that offsets the pain of life, the discord of life and the confusion of life.

It is to renew the Sacred and to restore people's awareness of the Sacred that God sends New Messages into the world. It is not just to affect human history. It is not simply to give humanity a new awareness, or to set in motion a greater set of events that can alter the course of human history. God's New Messages are designed to do these things, but fundamentally they are here to restore the Sacred. They are here to offset people's confusion and disassociation from the Sacred.

For what is Sacred becomes profane, becomes idols and rituals and beliefs and oppression. The Sacred now has been denigrated into a mechanism of control over people, a yoke and a harness for humanity, a demand, a set of rules that are inflexible and inhumane.

The Sacred has been lost. People are oppressed and impoverished. They fight with each other over what they think is sacred. They fight with each other over which of God's Messengers should be honored. They fight with each other over the history of their religion. They fight with each other over the resources of the world. They collide over their ideas, and the pain and the suffering of humanity are perpetuated and deepened. And the Sacred becomes lost to the people as an inspiration, as a mystery, as the invisible movement of God and God's emissaries.

So, at great intervals, a New Message from God must be sent into the world. Here there is no final prophet because the needs of humanity and the needs of the soul within each person call for the Sacred.

Without this, you are intelligent animals, so intelligent that you are aware of your future and your mortality, so intelligent that you suffer to a far greater degree than anything else in nature. But the Sacred lives with you. Without it, life is barren, a desert—without fulfillment, without a sense of permanence, without peace, without resolution. The Earth and the universe are cold and unforgiving. Without the Sacred, part of you is forever unfulfilled, a deeper part of you, the part of you that waits to be discovered.

Call nothing sacred. No place. No person. No book. No temple. No church. No mosque. Approach them with reverence, with respect, but do not call them sacred. For what is Sacred is so much greater. It is to take you beyond the world, while you are in the world, so that you can be in the world, but not of the world.

This is what gives you the power and the connection to God. Of course, it is mysterious because it existed before the world. It will exist after the world. That is why you cannot see it and hear it and hold it in your hands.

To experience this, you must learn to be still. And you must take the Steps to Knowledge, the deeper Mind that God has placed within you—where God's Movement can be experienced, where God's Wisdom can be experienced, where God's Will and Presence in your life can be experienced.

You do not have to be religious to have this experience. You do not have to believe in one religion to have this experience. Religion can be helpful here if it is understood as a pathway to the Sacred. But if religion is only a convenience, only something you feel you must be obedient to, only a social convention or a political requirement, it has lost its real value to you.

But for those who are not religious, who do not have a religious faith, who do not follow a prescription or a defined pathway, the Sacred is available to them as well. If they can experience this and feel the movement of this in their lives, it will relieve them of their grievances, their hostility, their anguish, their trepidation, their fear of life, their fear of themselves, their fear of others and their fear of God.

What else could God give you that would be greater than this—this great relief, this great affirmation, this great confirmation that you are sent here from beyond the world to give something very specific and very simple to the world?

To follow this is to move with what is sacred. It is to feel it moving your life. Whether you are religious or not, you are having a sacred experience.

It is more difficult for the rich to experience the Sacred because they have made so many other things sacred. It is hard for the poor to experience the Sacred because they are hungry. They are needy. They do not have what they need to sustain themselves, and so they believe in magic and miracles because they need a miracle to survive. They need something they cannot see to help them. [In this] it is easier for them to experience the Sacred.

But here, again, the Sacred is what is permanent—beyond the needs of the day, beyond wealth and splendor, beyond the pangs of hunger.

If humanity could realize this, it would bring an end to war. It would bring about the ability to cooperate and to unite. It would create a more genuine and common set of values. It would mean that religion would not be used as a pretext for war, as a tool of the state, as something that divides humanity and sets it in conflict with itself. There would be no argument over which book is sacred, which prophet is sacred, which Messenger is greater than the other Messenger. You would either experience what is sacred, or you would not.

God feeds you through the Sacred. If you are not fed, you are hungry. The soul is starving. Even if you are living in splendor, even if you have everything and the freedom to travel, your soul is forever hungry, and that is why you are so dissatisfied.

God feeds you at a different level, at the level of the soul, because here is where your life becomes real and meaningful, has purpose, has a direction, because you are moving with what is sacred, and you have not assigned the sacred to any other thing.

Possessions are either useful or not. They either help you or they do not. They have value in what they serve. Perhaps you need a lot to carry out your purpose in this world. Perhaps you need little or nothing. The value of things here is associated now with a greater purpose, with serving the Sacred, without becoming sacred themselves.

Even your body—do not call it sacred. But it can serve the Sacred. Only God really knows how this can be done fully. For you to know this, you must follow the deeper Intelligence that God has placed within you, where the movement of the Sacred can be experienced and expressed.

Every true artist knows this. Every person who is really creative knows this. They know they are the vehicle for something more mysterious. It is not just that they do phenomenal or unique tasks. There is something moving them that is the source of their creation or their art or their music—their inspiration.

The greatest gift is to share what you do in service to the Sacred—without calling your actions sacred, without calling your places sacred, without calling your books sacred. For what is sacred is what is permanent. That is what makes it sacred.

The Fire of Knowledge that is burning within you is generating the commitment and the courage and the conviction to make a real contribution to the world. This is like a Sacred Fire. You cannot put it out. You can only lose sight of it. God has put it there.

Otherwise, you would just become lost in the world, swept away, swept away by everything—by your passions, your difficulties, the problems of survival, the demands of others, the great and tragic movements of humanity and civilization. You would become lost to the world.

So God has placed Knowledge and the Fire of Knowledge within you. So even if you become lost, you are still connected. Even if you become confused, even if your life is denigrated, you are still connected to the Sacred.

Here you use your temple, your church, your mosque, your sacred place, the beauty of nature, your remembrances to serve the Sacred. Now they have meaning and value. They are not sacred, but they are serving the Sacred. That is their value. You pass through them like the wind. They have a greater service and they have a greater value, for they serve the Sacred, for you serve the Sacred.

Here there is no religious tyranny. Here there is no religious conflict. Here religion becomes a pathway to the Sacred, not the sacred itself. Here every pathway to the Sacred has value, if it is truly applied. There is no condemnation.

Here your ideas of Heaven and Hell fall away, for what is Heaven without the Sacred? And Hell is living without the Sacred. That has already been your experience. There are worse Hells. There are greater degrees of suffering and disassociation. But the Sacred remains, calling you to return.

Here you are freed from the past. Here you are freed from the beliefs of the past. Here you are freed from your aggression. Here you are freed from your hatred and your unforgiveness. It is all because of the Sacred that this is possible.

Return, then, to what is permanent and what is real. You cannot identify it. You cannot give it a place, a date or a name. To do so is to lose sight of it.

God has placed Knowledge within you so that the Sacred may move in your life and so that you may come to experience it even in your current set of circumstances. This is the greatest gift, and this is the source of your redemption. For the Sacred will give you a new life. It is life, the life that God created.

CHAPTER 4

GOD'S ANCIENT COVENANT
WITH HUMANITY

As revealed to
Marshall Vian Summers
on September 20, 2011
in Boulder, Colorado

Throughout history, humanity has made covenants with God, often thinking that it is God's Covenant that they are creating. These have varied according to the sacred Covenant that God has always made. For human understanding can never encompass the Divine awareness. And human ethics and human law can never mirror perfectly the Divine awareness, for it is far too great and mysterious, extending far, far beyond the realm and the reach of the intellect.

People want to have a concrete understanding, but God is mysterious. And what God has put within you to follow is mysterious. And while you are in the world, your greater life beyond the world is mysterious.

Therefore, the Mystery is a fundamental and essential part of your life, greater than you currently realize. It stands as the greater aspect of your reality. It represents your origin and your destiny beyond this world, the mystery of your relationships, the deeper inclinations, the mystery of the power of Knowledge, the greater Intelligence that the Creator has given to you, which is waiting to be discovered.

While human ethics and covenants have varied and human understanding has evolved, God has created a sacred Covenant with humanity. This Covenant has not really changed, so it is not correct to say that it is new though it may be new to your understanding. For the Covenant was established long before this world existed, long before there was a human race, long before there was a human history. The Covenant was established at the beginning of time, at the emergence of the Separation at the beginning of the physical universe. It is applicable not only to human beings, but to the billions and billions and billions of other races in the universe that are also part of Creation.

The Covenant is so essential and so fundamental to your nature, your Being and your purpose in the world that it can be overlooked or missed. For people's creation of a covenant with God has to do with their circumstances, their temperament, their history and how they perceive their future and their situation in life. But God's Covenant is far beyond this, for it has to be true in countless situations, in countless different races, in countless different worlds because the God of your world is also the God of the Greater Community of life in the universe.

The sacred Covenant is fundamental to all life. It was not specifically created for humanity, for there are countless races in the universe. It was not aligned to one specific religion or religious understanding, for there are countless religions in the universe.

That is why God's New Revelation is so very new because it takes you beyond the boundaries of this one world, opening you to the panorama of life in countless forms because who you are and where you have come from accounts for all of Creation, not simply one little aspect of it.

The Covenant, then, is not a Covenant with one people, or one nation, or one period of history, or one religion, or one part of the world. It is not tied to human philosophy, ethics or understanding. It is more fundamental than this. It must hold true in all dimensions for all races of beings who are living in Separation in the physical reality.

The Covenant, then, in one sense is very simple, but to live it and to live according to it requires great care. It requires real self-honesty. It requires a deeper discernment and a careful consideration of one's life and the lives of others.

The solution to the Separation was given at the beginning of time. It is not a problem for God. It is your problem. It is your dilemma as to what voice within you you will follow, and your desire and capacity to experience a greater and expanding truth and reality.

People want simple definitions. They do not want to have to work very hard. They want everything laid out for them because they are lazy and do not realize that they have to produce real effort and consideration and discernment to recognize that which is fundamental to their nature and purpose here.

The miracle of the Covenant, God's sacred Covenant, is that each person's purpose and destiny emanates from it. So while it is uniform and consistent throughout the universe, its manifestations are beyond count and comprehension. It is like life abundant flowing from the same fundamental soil and reality.

This certainly is beyond human comprehension, but it is not beyond human experience. You experience the Covenant every time you engage with the deeper Intelligence that God has created within you, which represents the part of you that has never left God and is still living according to God's Covenant.

So you may ask, "What is this Covenant? Explain it to me." And We say, God has put Knowledge within you, a perfect guiding Intelligence. God has given you a deeper conscience, which is part of this deeper Intelligence. God has sent you into the world to serve in a unique capacity in certain situations, engaging with certain individuals in certain circumstances.

At this moment, you do not fully understand what all this means or what is required or where it will all take place. It is only at the end of life looking backwards that you can see whether you have made this primary engagement in the world or not, that the primary engagement in the world is based on the deeper engagement with Knowledge within yourself, an Intelligence that exists beyond the realm of your intellect, beneath the surface of the mind. You are here to serve the world and to overcome your conflicts, your dilemmas and to a certain extent the dilemmas of your culture and existence in this particular world. Knowledge enables you to do this because it is part of Creation.

So it is not correct to say that "God is telling me this," or "God is telling me that," or "I am going here because God wants me to go here," or "I am doing this because God wants me to do this," or "I should choose this over that because God wants me to." It is more accurate to say that you are doing these things or basing these decisions upon the guidance and presence of Knowledge within yourself.

Knowledge, then, interprets the Will and the Presence of God and is able to translate that into decisions and actions and the awareness of things to avoid and things to approach, things to consider and things that you should not consider. How this functions is entirely beyond human speculation because it exists beyond the surface of the mind—the mind that you think with, the worldly mind, the mind that is informed by your culture and your education, your temperament and your circumstances.

To gain a greater freedom in life is to follow the power of Knowledge because this liberates you in a practical and meaningful way from many of the constraints of life in the world, the problems of relationships and the dilemmas and seemingly irresolvable difficulties that life in the world and in all worlds produces.

Do not think that traveling to another planet that seems to have resolved some of the problems you face today is going to be fundamentally better because freedom, individual freedom, is rare in the universe and is very difficult to establish and to maintain in the presence of other nations that are not free. This is part of gaining a Greater Community awareness, which is part of God's New Revelation for humanity.

The New Revelation presents the Ancient Covenant, which is that you experience God's Presence and Power through Knowledge within yourself. You experience God's Presence and Power in others through Knowledge within them, resonating with Knowledge within yourself.

You are here to serve the world because you were sent here to serve. Your enlightenment is always relative because you are living in Separation. But certainly the degree to which you can follow Knowledge, and have your life shaped by Knowledge, and directed by

Knowledge will determine the elevation of your mind and awareness, and the quality of your life and of your primary relationships.

God makes the way simple, but when the way is simple, it is demanding. It does not have countless exceptions. It is not fraught with preferences and negotiation. But it is difficult to understand if all you are using is your intellect to comprehend greater things, for the intellect was not created to comprehend greater things. It is the mechanism of the mind to deal with the practicalities of life and things of far less importance and scope. To go beyond this, you must engage with Knowledge.

You are also in the world to develop wisdom and to learn wisdom from others, the wisdom that is compassionate and gracious, but that is very sharp and clear, powerful and effective. You were born with Knowledge, but not with wisdom. And to live successfully in this world or any world, you will need to garner wisdom that is relative to that world, to your world.

God's New Revelation provides wisdom from the Greater Community, beyond what humanity has ever had to establish for itself. A marvelous and rare gift this is to prepare you for your future in the Greater Community, which is now upon you, to prepare you to engage with intelligent life in the universe, which is already upon you, exhibiting itself in dangerous and hazardous ways in the world today.

Your fundamental responsibility to God is to take the Steps to Knowledge; to learn to follow Knowledge and to discern Knowledge from the other voices in your mind; to listen to Knowledge in others, to search for it amongst all the opinions, attitudes and beliefs of people around you. Your fundamental responsibility is to have Knowledge reshape your life, which represents a deeper honesty within yourself. This is what it means to be true to yourself—not to your ideas or beliefs or preferences, not to your attitudes or cultural position, but to your deeper nature, which is represented by Knowledge and the emphasis of Knowledge within you.

God saves the separated through Knowledge. God redeems the separated through Knowledge. Not just human beings, but countless other races that are so very different from you—different in environment; different in belief; different in history; different in ethics, attitudes and associations. Only the genius of the Creator would have such a comprehensive Plan for redemption.

This, of course, makes all your absolute religious ideas very relative in the context of the Greater Community. That is why you cannot definitively discern the Will of God and try to apply that generally or in an absolute fashion to anything or anyone around you. But you are charged to take the Steps to Knowledge, and this is made very clear in God's New Revelation for humanity, which is now being given to the world—a Revelation unlike anything humanity has experienced before, a Revelation greater than anything that has been given for over a millennium. It is new in so many ways, and yet ancient and unchanging in others.

God's sacred Covenant with humanity is God's sacred Covenant with the universe. In this way, God does not have to be overly concerned and involved in your daily affairs. So when people say that God told them to do this or to do that, or God brought them this or took them away from that, really, if they are being honest, if their experience is true, they are talking about their engagement with Knowledge.

The Lord of all the universes is not involved in this way because the Lord of all the universes is so intelligent. The calamities of life, the natural disasters, the plagues, the wars, the great misfortune of living in Separation, the great predicaments of living in Separation, separate from your Source, following your surface and worldly mind alone—that is not created by God.

Look at the conditions of your world. You are given a paradise, and you are destroying it as quickly as your technology will allow. You are crushing your future. You are using up your natural inheritance. You are altering the world so significantly that it may become uninhabitable in the future. Do not think you are going to hop on some spacecraft and go somewhere else in the universe. Inhabited worlds such as yours have been long inhabited by races far more powerful than you.

That is why God's Covenant deals with the here and the now and with the decisions that each person makes, the choices they make, what they value, what they adhere to, what they respond to. This is where God's fundamental Covenant has overarching power in determining the future not only of an individual's life and circumstances, but of humanity as a whole.

For the future of humanity is being made by countless decisions, not simply by leaders of nations, but by every person, individually and collectively. And what informs that decision? Is it the power and the presence of Knowledge? Or is it the will, the fear and the ambitions of the individual? Clearly, humanity's foolishness, its stupidity, its errors, its tragedies, its conflicts all arise out of this fundamental problem of what informs the decisions of each person involved.

This is how God's Covenant is applicable in all situations. It is not that God has a different law or rule for this and a different law and rule for that. While you may be bound and even required to follow certain precepts and principles according to law and ethics of your given culture and nation, that is fine as long as it does not violate your fundamental relationship with Knowledge, which represents your Covenant with God.

Here your deeper conscience, not your social conscience, the deeper conscience becomes your ultimate judge of what must be done or not done. Said in another way, God's Covenant requires you to be fundamentally honest with yourself and true to your deeper nature.

While it is fine and necessary for nations to create ethics and principles and laws governing behavior to maintain social order and to mitigate the errors that will surely arise, and to at least idealistically or in principle create a just system, it is the conscience, the deeper conscience of the individual, that We speak of here today.

To engage with that conscience, you must be very honest. You must set aside your fears and your preferences long enough to know what is true at a deeper level. But this is difficult for people, for they have never exercised this very sufficiently, except for rare individuals in rare situations. So that is why God's New Revelation provides the Steps to Knowledge to give each person the opportunity to build a fundamental relationship and association with the power and presence of Knowledge within them.

Here you cannot make absolute beliefs because Knowledge may make one person to do one thing and tell another person not to do that. You cannot say, "My belief is the Will of God." Because the Will of God is manifesting itself in countless ways, working through individuals from the inside out, how can you predict what is absolutely correct for everyone? You cannot. It is dishonest. It is foolish. And it ends up being destructive to the lives of people.

The separated are reclaimed through Knowledge. The wicked are prepared for Heaven. Hell is where you are now, at least one level of Hell. You can go into a deeper Hell, a deeper state of Separation, but in the end, God will reclaim all of Creation.

It is because of the Covenant, you see. You cannot destroy Knowledge within yourself. You can divorce yourself from it. You can run from it. You can seal it off. You can deny it or disbelieve its presence and power. You can do everything you can to avoid your deeper conscience, but you cannot erase it. It is with you always. It was with you before you came into the world. It will be with you when you leave this world.

To engage with Knowledge while you are here is the real meaning of spirituality and spiritual development. To take the Steps to Knowledge is the core and fundamental action. Given in whatever religious tradition it may be manifest, it represents the fundamental spiritual practice. Believing in God or believing in a human ideology of God or trying to emulate what that teaching prescribes will not really be effective if you cannot gain a fundamental relationship with Knowledge. You are still separate from God. You are still functioning from your ideas, driven by fear—fear of loss, fear of failure, fear of deprivation, fear of God, fear of death, and so on and so forth.

That is why many people who consider themselves to be very pious in their religious faith are still not close to God because they have not made the fundamental connection with Knowledge within themselves. They have substituted their beliefs, their fundamentalism, their religious scriptures for their fundamental relationship with Knowledge. They have missed the mark. They are relying upon the wrong thing.

They are afraid of the Mystery, which is the source and meaning of their life. They want everything to be explained. They do not want to have to live with questions. They only want to use answers. They are afraid of themselves. They are afraid to go beneath the surface of the mind. They are afraid of God's Covenant, which supersedes their beliefs in all situations.

Many people claim to have a "natural religion," but it ends up becoming very unnatural because they have substituted their primary and primal relationship with Knowledge with a set of beliefs, an ideology, a system of thought or a religious institution. Belief now becomes their main focus instead of a deeper experience that transcends the limits of belief and is far more powerful, strong and permanent than any belief could ever be.

That is why there is a great difference between the manifestation of religion and all of its great edifices and pronouncements, its admonitions, its ideology, its cosmology, its theology and the Mystery that lives within each person, waiting to be discovered.

But people still need a structure, and that is why the New Message provides its ethics and gives a framework for participating in the world. But the framework is open. It is not absolute because Knowledge is working in different ways, in different people, to achieve the same goal and the same end.

When you leave this world and return to your Spiritual Family, who have been watching you in the world, they will ask you, "Did you achieve what you set out to achieve?" In that moment, you will not be encumbered by belief. For when you leave this world, you will not have any beliefs. But you will know intrinsically if you accomplished your tasks and objectives or not. Here there is no judgment. There is no condemnation. There is only the perfect Knowledge that you must try again.

How very different this is from people's notion that God is going to dispel all human error in the end, for God did not create human error, and therefore it must be uncreated by those who created it. But this would be impossible unless you had the power and presence of Knowledge within yourself. For only it can overcome evil. Only it can guide one in even the most complicated and difficult set of circumstances. Only it can make the right choice in every situation and choose the right people to be with. Only it can tell the difference between what is good from what only looks good.

This is God's Covenant. Mysterious it is, powerful, very difficult to articulate in words. Very difficult to create a new theology describing what Knowledge will do in all people, in all situations, in all circumstances, for this cannot be done. Instead, religion must create a framework, an ethical and practical framework that honors the fundamental spiritual practice of taking the Steps to Knowledge and encourages people in this direction and provides the wisdom of this era and of the ages to assist people in engaging with the power and the presence that lives within them, which exists beyond the realm and the reach of the intellect.

This is the difference between a saint and a scholar, you see. Scholars interpret, but it does not mean that their range of experience is very great. At best, they garner wisdom from the present and the past and bring it forth into the world's circumstances today. At worst, they become the scribes of ideology and the prosecutors of humanity.

There are important things to follow and not follow, and they are prescribed in God's New Revelation. They are general in the sense that they apply to most people and most situations and are very reliable. But you still have to make the deeper engagement with Knowledge. If you bypass this, then you put yourself in a position where you cannot receive God's Grace, Power and Presence except very incrementally and very infrequently.

God's essential Covenant says you can be separate, but only for a time, and in time. In the end, you are still part of Creation and will return. How different this is from the covenants that are proclaimed and established in humanity's religious institutions, and institutions of other races in the universe who have the same problems with the deeper engagement that you do.

There are no enlightened races of beings in the universe, or they would not be in this stage of reality. Everyone is dealing with the problems of Separation. And while there are wise individuals, and sometimes wise leaders of nations, everyone has the same fundamental problem. It is the problem not only of survival and security in a changing physical reality; it is the problem of what one will follow, and what others will follow within themselves and between each other.

If people in the world could become closer to Knowledge, then the commitment to follow certain resolutions would be far stronger than they are today. People would make sacrifices to do what is right. People would make decisions to do what will work. People would invest in the future and not simply try to live for the moment, like locusts upon the land.

You would have problems, but far fewer than you have today. And you would be building the foundation for a better future instead of trying to re-enact the past. You would preserve the world's resources instead of exhausting them. For this world is all you have, and what your children and their children will have in the future will be dependent upon what you can preserve and secure today.

Do not think you can go into the universe to gain that which you have depleted or destroyed here on Earth, for worlds such as yours are rare, and they are well protected. They are coveted by many.

This is part of growing up—ceasing to be a reckless race, an adolescent race, a destructive race. You would end war when you realized that you have to preserve the world and protect yourself against intervention from the Greater Community. It would change entirely your understanding of your situation and what would motivate you to do what is really correct and productive.

It is all based upon what informs the individual—the power and presence of Knowledge and God's Covenant with all life.

CHAPTER 5

THE PURPOSE OF RELIGION

As revealed to
Marshall Vian Summers
on July 20, 2009
in Antakya, Turkey

At this time and place, it is important to speak about the purpose of religion. Religion is part of the human experience, and any attempts that have been made to eradicate it or to minimize it have proven to be unsuccessful.

For you cannot deny the reality of the human spirit. You cannot deny the fundamental reality that there is a greater spiritual need in people that must be expressed.

But like all things in the world, that which is natural and essential can become distorted, misaligned and misused, allied with other purposes, particularly when these natural impulses become connected with governments and powerful forces in society.

Simply said, the purpose of religion is to cultivate the desire and the capacity to experience the Divine Presence in one's life. All teachings and rituals, whether within large institutions or within the privacy of one's home, are for this purpose. And the desire and capacity to experience the Divine Presence are to bring one to the power of Knowledge that the Creator of all life has placed within each human heart.

Yet when you look about, either at home or in foreign lands, you will find there is a great poverty, a great poverty in that people's lives are not demonstrating this Presence and the power of this Knowledge. The look of disappointment and dissatisfaction, the sense of regret in the older people, the sense of hopelessness and discouragement in the young are evidence that this power and this Presence are not being experienced.

Religion has become now a yoke and a harness for people, requiring them to believe along certain prescribed lines of thought and to behave along certain prescribed lines of behavior. But this is far from the essence of what religion is really for. To require, either through inducement or threat, for people to adhere to a certain system of belief does not represent the essence and the purpose of religion. Yet that is what is so manifest in the world today.

Religion has become another form of government—a form of government that seeks power and domination, a form of government that seeks to overcome its competing rivals, the competing agendas of other religious traditions and faiths. And so there is a contest and a kind of war exerted between the most radical elements of these systems of belief. But this is not what religion really is.

The Creator of all life has initiated all the world's religions, but they have all been altered by people and governments, by cultures and traditions and by the competition for power in the world. That is why there are so many people today in the world who, though they have genuine spiritual needs and yearnings, are so put off by the manifestations of religion as it has become.

Where can you find the cultivation of one's inner life? Where is the emphasis on recognizing, following and embracing the power and the presence of Knowledge within the individual? Where is the emphasis on developing and encouraging the individual's capacity and desire to experience the Mystery of the Divine Presence—a Mystery that defies all religious teachings and conventions?

Where are such things being encouraged for the individual? You visit the church or the temple or the mosque and what is presented but an emphasis on upholding the ideology of religion, the institutions of religion, the demands of religion? This emphasis is out of context and out of relationship with the essential purpose of religion.

In essence, all religion is to teach The Way of Knowledge, to bring the individual into the direct experience of Knowledge, the deeper Mind beyond the intellect, the Mind that God has provided each person to guide them, to protect them and to lead them to a greater life and expression in the world.

But you do not hear this emphasis. Instead, there is the encouragement to believe, to adhere, to follow the prescriptions of a religious tradition, however illogical and unreasonable those prescriptions may be within the context of modern life. And this is called "the Word of God," God's Will for humanity.

Of course, there is great competition between competing powers over who has the ultimate and final claim of God's Will and prescription for humanity. It is as if the unreligious have taken over the business of religion for their own purposes. Never having realized its essential purpose and meaning, they have turned it into something else. It is like now a political party and, of course, religion has political aims as well.

This is so far apart from God's initial impulse and intention for religion—to keep Knowledge alive in the world, to teach The Way of Knowledge, to encourage human responsibility and ethical behavior, not simply as a prescript or as a requirement for admission into Heaven or some other exalted future state.

It is really a denial of the natural integrity and natural ethics that will arise with the person who has experienced this power and presence of Knowledge and is guided by its wisdom and its grace. These individuals, no matter what part of the world they reside, no matter what tribe or group or culture they come from, will all uphold the same values because these are the values of Knowledge.

So you have a world that seems deeply religious, but is not practicing and emphasizing what religion is really for. And given the submission and oppression of peoples throughout human history, whatever sacred intent has been maintained has been maintained only for the elite, for the monastic, for the adept.

As a result, God's true Messengers have had to break the chains of convention, have had to teach in opposition in the face of the prevailing religious beliefs and attitudes. They have had to become rebels and reformers, counteracting humanity's tendency to turn what is sacred into what is profane.

What is the intent of the true Messenger but to evoke the spiritual Fire in the individual and to bring them in contact with the deeper conscience that exists within them—a conscience that is not the product of social conformation or social expectation, but a deeper conscience that is innate and essential to the human life?

THE PURPOSE OF RELIGION

So you have a world that is religious, but knows not of religion. You have a world where religious institutions and their advocates clash and compete with one another, not realizing that the Source of their faith is the same. They will have people demanding and expecting adherence to ideas and beliefs and admonitions, but who themselves have never received the real initiation into the mystery and the power of the Presence.

Religion has become concrete. It has become political. It has become an economic and social power that seeks to preserve its status and its power at whatever cost. So now those who are truly responding to religion's true purpose now find themselves in exile, now find themselves heretics and visionaries following the Mystery—a Mystery that has been lost to so many in the religious orders and institutions.

It is as if religion has become the enemy of what religion is really for. It is now the religion of the state, religion of tradition, religion of history, religion of fixed ideas, fixed beliefs and exclusive claims of authority. So far this is from the desire and intent of the Creator to keep Knowledge alive in the world.

In certain cases, religion has become the enemy of Knowledge, declaring that only God has Knowledge and that people are foolish and must be corralled like animals, must be programmed and conditioned to believe—to believe things that are incredible and impossible, to believe things that run counter to the deeper experience that people have, things that are apart from the real mystery and the profound experience that is the essence of what religion really is.

Throughout the ages, the mystics, the wise amongst them, have kept this Power and this Presence alive, but they were the outcasts, at the margin of religious institutions. They were the rebels and the reformers who, though disapproved of or distrusted by their authorities, actually gave life and substance and meaning to the empty religious practices that prevailed in human society.

So what does this mean for you? This means that there is a greater power in your life, a greater mystery in your life, and that your connection to God is through Knowledge, the deeper Intelligence that God has placed within you, an Intelligence that is beyond the realm and the reach of your intellect. This power is calling to you, and your response to it represents the deepest need of your soul—a need that is deeper than the need for survival and gratification, for education and opportunity, for friendship and partnership.

To find this need, you must realize that what the world is providing is inadequate. It meets social and psychological needs. It meets practical needs. But it does not meet the real need of the soul. That requires an engagement of an extraordinary kind.

The Creator of all life, of course, understands this predicament—that religion has become the problem and not the answer, that religion has become the impediment and not the pathway, that the true purpose and emphasis of religion has been lost in so many ways that now only a very wise and exceptional teacher within a faith tradition can speak to the Mystery and the Power and refer to the deeper conscience within the individual.

But such teachers are rare. They represent the minority of those who claim ecclesiastical powers and authorities. For how can you be allegiant to the church or the mosque or the temple if your greatest allegiance is to Knowledge, which represents your allegiance to God? And if God is not bound by human thought, human philosophy and human theology, then you as a follower of Knowledge will not be bound by these things either. This makes you free and uncontrollable. This makes you perceptive and more incorruptible. This makes you question the value of religious authority and the ethics and behavior of religious institutions—all things that religious institutions are prone to resist and to repress.

Therefore, it is necessary that you come back to what is essential, to the initial impulse and power of religion—not the religion of the state, not the religion of the traditional institutions necessarily, but to something much purer that can exist within them and beyond them.

Beware of beliefs that seem set in stone. Beware of proclamations of exclusive privilege or authority by religious leaders. Recognize that there are people who are freedom oriented and there are people who are control oriented. The control oriented are afraid of freedom, and they are afraid of Mystery because they do not believe in the essential goodness of the human spirit. They have lost their faith in humanity and have placed all their faith in their ideology and the prescriptions that they believe have come from God.

But God has only given recommendations through the great teachers, not rules—recommendations for living, guidelines for living to help people orient their lives correctly and productively and beneficially.

Therefore, to find your real connection, you must come to learn The Way of Knowledge, for at the heart of every religion, there is The Way of Knowledge. This is not the way of belief. This is not the way of obedience. This is not the way of blindly following prescriptions and precepts and admonitions of religious leaders and institutions. It is finding the power and presence of Knowledge within you and learning over time and through instruction how to discern this power and presence from the other impulses and compulsions that exist within you as an individual.

God's Purpose in the world is to keep Knowledge alive so that human freedom, human justice and human compassion may be kept alive in the world. God's Purpose is not to exalt religious leaders or institutions, or to crown one over another. These are human creations and not God creations, and they are fallible and prone to corruption as a result.

God has provided a New Message into the world to clarify this picture and to provide a clear pathway for those who seek to have the real experience. They can have this experience within their religious traditions or outside of them.

God's New Revelation may conflict with political ideology and longstanding beliefs, but that is what happens when what is pure is contrasted with what has been altered and adapted.

God is not bound by human creations, human beliefs and admonitions. God only provides what is real and essential to ignite the human heart and to give each individual a foundation for being inner directed rather than outer directed.

Here your imam or your rabbi or your priest can help you if they are guided by Knowledge. But they will hinder you if they are not. You must learn to see the difference.

Religions are institutions that have to be maintained and protected. They are in competition with each other, so none of them that exist in the world today can really foster human peace and human unity. For they all claim special privileges, and only those few individuals within them that support a great ecumenical movement and the acceptance of all world's religions can counteract this competition, which is inherently divisive and destructive.

In these words, We speak to the human heart, not to the intellect that wants to have everything figured out and wants to adhere to its notions, its beliefs and its traditions.

There is nothing wrong with a tradition if it fulfills the basic purpose of religion, which is to inspire and expand people's desire and capacity to experience the Presence of God and to connect them with the deeper Intelligence that God has placed within them that will be essential for their success and their well-being in the world. This is much more important than the teachings of the founder of a religious tradition. It is much more important than the religion's official declarations of belief or doctrine.

People celebrate and worship and repeat endlessly the lives of the great teachers, but can they really live the lives that these teachers promoted? It is not merely human behavior that is important, for people can behave well for all the wrong reasons. People can fall in line with each other for social advantage, for economic advantage and to achieve social status and acceptance. But this is not religion.

You who seek to know your greater purpose in the world and the greater meaning of your life, this means you are a religious person. Whether you belong to a church or a mosque or a synagogue or any other religious organization, that is secondary.

Promoting a religious ideology in the world does not represent supporting God's Will and Purpose here. It is only if this ideology and system of belief can meet the basic requirements of religion will they have real and lasting value and produce real benefit for people.

Likewise, no religious teaching should promote war and attack upon other groups. This represents competition for power between these groups, but this is not what religion is.

Religion is bringing you to God and to what God has placed within you to guide you, to protect you and to lead you to your great accomplishments in life. Anything beyond this is an invention, a human invention, an adaptation.

People will have to figure out what this means in terms of the application of law and the running of societies. God is not here to run societies or to carry out the intricacies of jurisprudence or the administration of the law.

God is pointing you to the Mystery, not to the manifestation. God is calling you into the Mystery, not prescribing the manifestation. If you want to have more saints in the world, if you want to have truly inspiring individuals in the world, if you want humanity to have a higher standard that is born not out of an oppressive regime, but out of a natural understanding, then you must guide people to the power of the Mystery.

Religion, you see, does not have an answer for every social and political problem, but it does give people access to the deeper Intelligence that can guide people effectively in meeting all these needs. Religion must be free of the state and it must be free of politics, which will only taint and corrupt it to the point where those who claim to be holy men will call for the execution of people.

This is the degree of distortion and aberrancy that has been established in the world today, and that is why there is a New Message from God—to restore the clarity and the purpose of religion and the meaning of spiritual practice and the nature of the Divine revelation that must happen within each person.

It is not enough to celebrate a great teacher's Revelation if you cannot find access to your own. It is not enough to worship a great teacher or emancipator unless you can find this power and this presence within your life, which will apply itself in far more mundane and simple day-to-day circumstances.

Here the contrast is significant and must be comprehended. If you want religion to be a thing, you will lose its essence and its meaning and turn it into something else that it was never meant to be. If you want to turn religion into a set of ideals and beliefs or a complex theology, you will lose what religion really is and what it is for.

To argue whether Jesus or Muhammad is the greatest teacher or provides the final word for humanity is so utterly ridiculous, and so far from the nature and intent of religion as God intended it to be that it represents a kind of pathetic diminishing and distortion of what religion really is.

To think that Muhammad gave the final Revelation is to misunderstand God's Purpose and Presence. For God has many more things to say to the world, particularly at this great turning point when humanity is facing a declining world, a world of declining resources, when humanity is facing the reality of contact with intelligent life in the universe—two great events that none of God's previous Revelations are meant to address or that can address sufficiently and reasonably.

Religion has become overlaid with ideas, beliefs, institutions, laws and requirements that have become repressive to the people or abhorrent to people who are freedom loving. They do not meet the deeper need of the soul. That is why you must come back to what is essential, to what is real. The temple, the mosque, the church and the tribal place of worship are the places to honor the Mystery and to evoke the Presence and the Power.

The Way of Knowledge, which is at the heart of all the world's religions, must become its essential teaching, instead of a focus for clerics and monastics and exceptional individuals only. This is the challenge before you, or religion will be part of the problem for humanity and not its essential means of reconciliation, inspiration and a high ethical awareness. Let this be your understanding.

CHAPTER 6

GOD'S NEW MESSAGE FOR THE WORLD'S RELIGIONS

As revealed to
Marshall Vian Summers
on January 23, 2015
in Jerusalem, Israel

Today We shall speak on God's New Revelation and the world's religions.

First, you must understand that God has initiated all the great religions of the world, and in each case has sent a Messenger from the Angelic Assembly to initiate these traditions at the outset.

All the great Messengers have come from the Assembly, so they are intrinsically united, you see. They have all been sent by the Source, your Source and the Source of all the world's religions.

But living in Separation, people have separated the religions from one another and even internally—separating everything that was meant to be united, misunderstanding the meaning and the value of the Messengers and what they were really presenting.

But this limitation is understood by God, for you cannot understand God's Greater Plan for the world living for the moment. Living in Separation, you cannot yet see the greater panorama of things. For each religion was meant to be a building block in humanity's development and evolution, preparing humanity for a future that would be unlike the past.

The great Revelations were given at pivotal times in human history, times not only of change and challenge, but times of great opportunity when these Revelations could spread. They were placed in certain places for this purpose, places where the Message could move beyond one tribe or one group or one nation, at times of opportunity greater than what anyone could see in the moment.

Here you must understand that the world's religions are all part of a Greater Plan. And while they are distinct from one another in certain ways, their distinction represents their unique contribution to the growing wisdom and compassion and ethics of the human family.

For God knows that not everyone can follow one teaching or one teacher or even one interpretation. Living in Separation, you do not yet have the skill and the development to do this. And if one interpretation is forced upon the people, it becomes a form of oppression and is counterproductive in that way.

What We are telling you here today is very different from how religion is regarded and used in this world and, in fact, how it is regarded and used throughout the universe. For all who live in the physical reality are living in Separation—separation from their Source and from the timeless reality from which all have come and to which all eventually will return. This is beyond human comprehension and certainly beyond any possibility of a religious understanding.

This greater understanding now of the unity of the world's religions, the unity of their Source and intention, is vital because they all must now play a part in building human cooperation to face a world in decline, a world of environmental disruption, a world of growing economic and social disruption—a reality that the human family has never had to face before; a reality created by humanity's misuse of the world and its contamination of your air, your water and your soils, which now has the power to undermine human civilization and create a human tragedy unlike anything that has ever been seen here before. Greater than all of your wars combined it is.

For the Great Waves of change are coming, and they have already begun. The world will become hotter. Crops will fail. Water will dry up or become flooded in certain places. The world's economy will be shaken by this. And the livelihoods of the people will be shaken by this.

That is why God has spoken again. And that is why God must address the condition of the world's religions because they are in contention with each other, and even internally divided. And religious violence is now growing in the world and will grow further as the Great Waves of change impact more and more people, depriving them of their security, depriving them of their foundation for living here.

The world's religions are all given as building blocks of human civilization. Each block is not like another. Each block is unique, bringing something unique to humanity's understanding and perspective. But to see this, you must see beyond your desire for Separation, where you try to make everything unique and separate to validate yourself and your ideas.

We are giving you the Will of Heaven here and how Heaven looks at the world's religions, as the spokes of a wheel, around the central axis of the Creator. They are all rivers moving towards the same sea.

They appear to be separate and unique in their features, in their landscapes, but they are all leading to the same outcome.

To see this, you will have to change your religious beliefs and adjust your understanding, for there is not one religion for all, for that can never be. God knows this even though the people are still confused.

There is no final Revelation because God has more to say to the world as humanity is now facing thresholds it has never had to face before, standing at the threshold of space, encountering others from the universe who are here in the world to undermine human authority and sovereignty here.

You are living in a condition never seen before in the history of human civilization. You are at a new juncture. And the world's religions cannot prepare you for this. They were not given for this purpose, given in antiquity.

A new building block must be given now to complete the picture and to carry it forward so that humanity may be prepared for its new future and to live in a new world environment, where human cooperation and unity will be necessary for humanity's survival and well-being.

God's New Revelation, therefore, must bring great correction and clarification and will challenge many of the fundamental ideas and beliefs that separate the world's religions and place them in contention with one another. For their fundamental unity is because of their Source and the intention of their Source in providing them at critical turning points for humanity.

They are all there, giving their unique service to humanity. And people are called to participate in one of them. For in this matter, you cannot simply create your own pathway, for the great pathways have been given.

But because they have been misused and misunderstood, subject to human adoption and corruption, many people have turned away in dismay and confusion and disappointment, seeing how the religions of the world have been used as banners of war, been used to suppress peoples cruelly, ignorantly, foolishly, against the Will of the Creator.

Many people have turned away from the traditions that are meant to serve them. And now people are lost, thinking they can create their own pathway, by borrowing from this or borrowing from that. But only God knows the way to return. You cannot create your own way, based upon human preference and human admonition.

People have been assigned to one of the great traditions, but now they are alienated from it, cast out into the world with all of its persuasions, its denigration, its harshness, its cruelty.

Therefore, great clarification must be brought to the world's religions or they will continue to divide humanity, each claiming to be exclusive, each claiming to have dominance or God's preference over the others, filled with ambitious people, adopted by governments for their own purposes.

Let it be understood, then, that religion can never be used as a banner of war or a justification for cruelty, torture, punishment or death. This all represents humanity's misuse of the great religions and the misunderstanding of their purpose in building human unity, human values and human ethics.

War and punishment are done for other reasons. Never claim that God justifies or has directed such things, for this is a grave misunderstanding. To harm others in the name of God is a crime against God, and God's Will and Purpose, and God's intention regarding the establishment of the great traditions.

You can see here from what We tell you today that this is very different from what people proclaim about their religion, what they believe or are taught to believe. For they have become corrupted, one and all, in certain ways.

For a Christian not to help a Muslim, or a Muslim not to help a Jew, or a Jew not to help a Hindu represents the core problem. Now religion is part of the problem and not part of the solution as it was intended, as it was always intended.

Fundamentally, all the religions are here to bring you to the Knowledge that God has placed within you to guide you and to begin a process of redemption that would be carried out step by step in your life and circumstances if you were able to follow this guidance correctly.

It will require great compassion and forgiveness. It will require for you to see your life and others in a different way and not fall prey to the seductions of hatred and discrimination.

There is always a distinction between the Will of Heaven and the understanding of people. But to bridge this gap within yourself, you must take the Steps to this Knowledge that We speak of. For it represents the part of you that has never left God and can receive the Will of God for you, specifically.

In this, you will not be in contention with others because Knowledge within you is not in contention with Knowledge in others.

It is the beliefs of the mind. It is the social and the religious conditioning of the mind. It is your preferences, your anger and your unforgiveness that stand in the way of this greater recognition, which would liberate you from so much of your suffering and sense of unworthiness.

So God must speak again to prepare you for the Great Waves of change coming to the world. God must speak again to prepare you for your encounter with a universe full of intelligent life, a non-human universe where freedom is so rare.

And God must speak again to bring correction and clarification to the world's religions so that they may have the chance to fulfill their true purpose and destiny here, which is to generate greater cooperation and unity, forgiveness and compassion amongst the tribes and nations of the world.

They are all meant to serve in this capacity in their unique ways and to provide unique perspectives and understanding to balance each other and to lead humanity back to their primary relationship with God.

Here you must understand that the Messengers are not gods. They all come from the Angelic Assembly. Half holy, half human they are, greater than any other person in the world in this respect. But you cannot worship them. You cannot appeal to them for favors and dispensations. This you must appeal to God directly.

All that We are telling you here today will require much consideration. And many people will reject these things to defend their beliefs and ideas and investment in their religious perspective or their social or religious position in society. They will be blind to the God that they proclaim that they follow.

For if you cannot receive God's New Revelation, what does that mean about your relationship with God? It means you have a relationship with humanity's understanding of God, but your relationship with God is not yet strong enough to override these things.

It is a great challenge at the time of Revelation. Whenever this has happened, perhaps once in a millennium, it is always a great challenge for the recipient.

Can they listen anew? Can they respond? Can they step beyond their beliefs and the things that circumscribe them? Do they have the heart and will to know the truth beyond human ideology?

For no religious understanding in the world can encompass the Purpose and Plan of God in this world, let alone the universe beyond you, a universe so great and vast your intellect is far too small to even comprehend it.

We are telling you these things so that the true purpose and initiation of the world's religions can be rekindled and rediscovered. But for this, you must follow the Knowledge that God has placed within you, for your mind is far too conditioned, far too afraid of change, far too limited by your conditioning, and for many people, far too oppressed by poverty and political and religious oppression in the world.

You must appeal to your deeper conscience that God has placed within you at the beginning. This is not to make you a great saint or avatar or a great messenger, but to enable you to discover your unique contribution and service to the world. Humble it will be. Specific it will be. It is meant for certain people and places and situations. At this moment, you cannot understand this. You can only follow the pathway that Knowledge will lead you into, and have the faith to do this, and have the self-respect to trust this within yourself and others.

For humanity to survive the Great Waves of change, for human civilization to remain intact and to grow and expand facing the Great Waves of change, for human freedom and sovereignty to be built and strengthened in the face of intervention from the universe around you, human cooperation and the cooperation of humanity's religious traditions must be re-established and renewed, beginning with you and your understanding, and your heart and mind.

Look not to others here, for you must bring yourself into alignment with this first. Do not blame and condemn nations and leaders no matter how ignorant they may appear to be, for you must bring your own house into order—your mind, your emotions, your beliefs, your grievances. Allow the healing of God's New Revelation to liberate you from that which oppresses you and keeps your mind small, living in darkness and confusion.

That is why the Revelation is focused on the individual. For everything that will happen in the future will be based upon the decisions of individuals and what informs those decisions. Will it be the power and presence of Knowledge within them? Or will it be the forces of persuasion in the world and the darkness of fear, anger and hatred?

The service and giving in the future will be so great. The need will be so great. There will be whole regions of the world where people will be forced to leave. Who will receive them? Who will accept them? They will no longer be able to provide for themselves, for their lands will become barren. And the seas will rise, engulfing their ports and cities in the future. It will be a human need and calamity on a scale never seen.

Do not think this is the Will of God. It is the consequence of how humanity has lived in this paradise that is now being turned into a hellish environment. Step by step, day by day, humanity is devouring the world as fast as possible, with no thought of the future, contaminating the air, the water and the soils, with no thought of the future, greedily, like locusts upon the land.

This is ignorance. This is foolishness. You can understand what We are saying here. You cannot just live for the moment. You have to prepare for the future in all things. You can understand what We are saying here.

The Will of Heaven is that the world's religions will all participate in the restoration of humanity, according to the needs of people, not just according to their philosophies or ideologies. Everyone must pitch in to save the ship upon which you all live, for that ship is now taking on water and listing to one side.

This is the purpose of all the world's religions—feeding people, caring for people, forgiving people, uniting people. There can be no violence or contention between the world's religions if they are understood correctly. These acts are a crime against God and God's Will and intentions for Earth, for you and for all peoples.

GOD'S NEW MESSAGE FOR THE
WORLD'S RELIGIONS

Humanity must band together to protect itself from the Great Waves of change that it has created and to prepare for its engagement, its hazardous engagement, with intelligent life from beyond the world.

You will not find this emphasis in the world's religions unless you search very deeply. You will not see this if you live for the moment only or have your eyes to the past. For religion must be vital today and tomorrow and must prepare itself for the welfare of humanity, understanding that God has created all the world's religions, and they have all been changed by man.

Now they must return to their Source and to the initial intention that created them and the intention that requires them now to each join in service to the welfare of the peoples of the world, not only their adherents, but all peoples. In this, they become true servants of the human family. In this, they return to their initial purpose—the purpose for which they were given.

Only God's New Revelation for the world has the Power of Heaven to do this. You may think such a thing is not possible, given where people are associating themselves and how they think and behave. But We are talking about the Will of Heaven here, which can alter the course of human destiny if it can be received, if it can be accepted by enough people in the world.

Many will fight against this, of course, because that always happens at times of Revelation. It all depends on who can receive the Will of Heaven now, standing at the threshold of a new world, standing at the threshold where humanity will have to choose to unite and to persevere, or to descend into endless chaos and self-destruction.

May you listen with your heart. May you open your mind for Revelation. May you accept that you were sent here for this purpose, to live in these times, to serve the world under these conditions and to prepare yourself and others for the great change that is coming.

This is the Will of Heaven, and within yourself, deep beneath the surface of your mind, you will know this to be true.

CHAPTER 7

RELIGIOUS FUNDAMENTALISM

As revealed to
Marshall Vian Summers
on September 23, 2014
in Boulder, Colorado

People living in Separation try to make everything fit Separation. They try to make their ideas, their activities, their beliefs and their emphasis in life function within the realm of living in isolation, being separated from God and their Source.

The Lord of all the universes, the Lord of all Creation, the Source of your life has established all the world's great religions. Even though they have been altered over time and changed through human adoption, corruption and misunderstanding, they are all meant to unite humanity. They are all meant to add dimensions to human civilization. They are all meant to prepare you for the future, for all the great Revelations are here to prepare you for the future.

Yet living in Separation, people, many people, make their religion the only religion, or the final religion, or the complete religion to the exclusion of all others. It is a human tendency, and it is associated with belief.

Belief is of the mind. It is not of the Spirit. Belief is useful and necessary to a point: to organize your thinking, to give your life focus and direction and orientation. But thinking, living in Separation, is never absolute. For where you are going and where you have come from is beyond the realm and the reach of the intellect.

To believe that your great spiritual teacher, the founder of your religion, is the only great teacher, or the final great teacher, is a fundamental mistake. If all the religions have been initiated by God and changed by man, then clearly it is a glaring mistake.

To think that God has nothing more to say to humanity as it faces the greatest challenges now in its entire history is a fundamental mistake. To think that the religions of antiquity can prepare you for life in the universe, or for living in a declining world, is clearly inappropriate. Yet many people hold to these ideas, base their lives upon these ideas, are willing to go to war with others over these ideas.

So the abuses of religion continue. They have been grievous over time because the Spirit of God is not being experienced.

Like the rivers leading to the sea, all religious traditions are to bring you back into wholeness and union with God. They each add a unique dimension to the understanding of being in the world and of living with a dual reality—the reality of your spiritual nature, which is embodied in what We call Knowledge, and your worldly identity that has been established through culture and through interaction with life here in the world.

You have this dual nature, you see. You are not one without the other. But your greater nature is not based upon ideology. It is not based upon religious belief or practice or tradition. It is beyond these things because God is beyond these things. And when you leave this world, you will be beyond these things. You will not have any beliefs. You will just be there, just like you were before you came into the world.

So people come into the world, and they become laden and imprinted with belief. And if they accept this, they become the advocates of belief, sometimes very mindlessly, simply because they are so heavily imprinted and conditioned to think a certain way, to hold certain ideas and beliefs and have certain opinions about their religion and tradition.

God does not care about these things. They are all expedient measures to bring you back into union with God. That is their purpose, you see, and to help organize your life so that you can live an ethical, wholesome and valuable life in the world.

It is a human tendency in all religious traditions, more pronounced in some than in others, to establish a firm and fixed idea about God, and about everything else. This occurs beyond religion because it is a primary human tendency living in Separation.

You base your ideas, your identity and your position in society, even your wealth and affluence, upon a fixed set of ideas. But you can never get to God with a fixed set of ideas because they blind you. They limit you. They make you judgmental and condemning of others. They can lead you to violence and conflict, repression and brutal condemnation of others. You cannot know your Source if this is your position, no matter how much tradition is behind you, for the traditions of religious error are as fixed as the traditions of religious truth.

It is what you listen to within yourself that is the fundamental issue here. If you base your identity on your ideas, then you will want your ideas to be fixed and immovable so you can have security regarding this. You will see all others who have different ideas as in competition with you or as a threat at some level, or you will just condemn them for being inferior or unholy—the disbelievers, the unbelievers—and you will judge them and condemn them to hell.

This is religion held by those who are living in Separation. It is incorrect from beginning to end because they do not understand the nature of God, or their relationship with God, or the fact that God will save everyone in the end, for this is the Plan of God.

God will save everyone in this world and in every world, in billions and billions of worlds—beings that are so different in appearance and orientation [from] you. For this is the Plan of God. It will take an enormous amount of time, of course, but time is nothing to God.

The great Messengers come bringing New Revelations at times of great significance, challenge and opportunity, to add to the growing understanding and to keep the spirit and the practice of your Divine faith intact and renewed as it grows cold and calcified in the ideas and minds of people.

Never rest upon your ideas and beliefs, or your mind will close and become dark, and you will just become another adversary in a world of adversaries. You will become partisan. You will have enemies. You will build your faith around your enemies. You will think that the enemies of God are your enemies, and you will assign [this] to people you do not like or understand.

God understands these things because you are living in Separation, and you have not yet found the natural Intelligence that God has put within you to follow. So you depend upon your ideas and the ideas of others and the consensus of thinking amongst nations and cultures and people. And you are as blind as can be, as a result.

RELIGIOUS FUNDAMENTALISM

You cannot see outside your little prison house of ideas that you defend, or tend to defend, so vigorously. You cannot see. You are imprisoned. It is the prison of the mind. It is the prison of fixed belief. You cannot learn anything new, really. You only try to fortify that which you believe and hold to be true.

The purpose of Revelation is to take you beyond belief, ultimately. It will use belief in the interim as a starting point, but you must go beyond this. You can never understand God, or how God works in the world, or who and what God is and your relationship with God at the level of belief.

Belief here is so limited. It is so self-serving. It is so conditioned by culture and religion around you. It can never encompass any greater reality, or greater truth about your life, and why you are here, and who sent you and what you must do next.

That is religion. Following the greater presence that God has given to you, the greater Intelligence called Knowledge—that is how you come back into union with God, through service and contribution in the world.

Worshipping God means nothing without this. Prostrating yourself in the mosque, the church or the temple means nothing without this service. God does not need worship. God is not like you. God is not insecure. God does not need to be praised. God is not like you in this regard.

People try to use God for favors and dispensations and use their belief to try to gain these things. But the Angelic Host who watches over this world is not moved by these things.

Religion is used by governments. It is used in a quest for power. It is used to dominate and suppress populations. It has been used throughout history as a banner of war and a banner of subjugation.

People make God into what they want God to be and what they believe God to be—a God like themselves, a God who has all the human tendencies, a God with great power, yes, but a God that in a way is rather tragic.

God is patient, so you must learn to be patient. God is tolerant, so you must learn to be tolerant. God is the Source of all the world's religions, so you must respect them all and learn of them to see their value and contribution.

God moves in the world working through people from the inside out. Therefore, you must listen for this in others.

God has put Knowledge within you to guide you, to bless you and to protect you, to prepare you for a greater life of service and fulfillment. You must take the Steps to this Knowledge. For that is the pillar and the true pathway of your faith, in whatever religious tradition you are functioning.

God does not condemn, so you must not condemn. God does not punish, so you must not punish mindlessly and heartlessly.

Your belief can never contain the Greater Plan of God or what your religion really means and why it was sent into the world. These things all exist beyond the realm and the reach of the intellect, really.

Having wonderful and fantastic notions is not going to bring you back into union with God or with the greater purpose that has sent you here and that is waiting to be discovered. This is what God responds to.

Dying for your beliefs, killing others for your beliefs is an abomination in the name of God. It is sickness. It is mental illness, affecting large populations of people.

The true believer in God does not do these things. The true faith is in the power and presence of Knowledge and in those who sent you and who watch over you, even now.

This is a Mystery. Everything of value comes from the Mystery. You must have the courage and the humility to enter the Mystery, to live with questions and not base your life upon answers, to go beyond the word, for the word is only the beginning of your journey back to God.

God is not here to take you out of the world but to bring you into the world with a greater purpose and meaning. But to allow God to help you, you must be willing to change your life and your ideas and depart from your old way of thinking and behaving.

This is the challenge, but this is also the liberation. For your old way of thinking and behaving, in nearly all cases, will bring you nowhere but despair and emptiness. And you will return to your Ancient Home with your mission unfulfilled and unrecognized.

There is no Judgment Day. There is no Hell and damnation. Why would God damn you or condemn you when God knows that without Knowledge, you can only be in error, trying to use your ideas and beliefs as pillars of truth when the greater truth is beyond them entirely?

God has sent a great Revelation into the world now, sent from the Angelic Assembly, it is. It is the most expansive ever given to this world, given at a time of profound need and great change. It is the greatest threshold in all of human history as humanity faces living in a declining world, as humanity faces a universe full of intelligent life. Your beliefs likely do not account for these things. And even if they did, they would not be complete.

You will need God to help you now, for humanity is very late in its preparation. Human belief, human religion, cannot prepare you for these two great thresholds. It is a reality in which humanity must unite to survive, must out of sheer necessity cooperate and end its ceaseless conflicts.

It is a time of great change in the thinking and the traditions of thinking that have been so determining of human thought and behavior in the past. It is a great restoration if it can be seen correctly. And it will be very challenging for all people to face and to accept. But there is no running away from the Great Waves of change that are coming to this world. And you cannot escape the fact that humanity is now being visited by dangerous forces from the universe.

These things are happening whether you are ready or not, whether you are willing or not, whether you are aware or not. They will alter the course of your life and the destiny of your children—a great danger, a great opportunity, for you and for all of the human family.

You must be willing to step out of your fixed beliefs—your political beliefs, your religious beliefs, your social beliefs—to re-engage with reality and to see that unless humanity can unite for its own protection and advancement, it will disintegrate and fall prey to foreign powers. This has happened countless times in the universe around you.

God knows what is coming over the horizon and the great hazards and risks ahead. And God knows the great opportunity, the greatest opportunity ever, for humanity to unite on its own behalf to protect human civilization, to restore the productivity of the world and to assure a future for humanity.

Religious fundamentalism will just fight and struggle, destroy and alienate. This is not the Will of the Creator. Religion is meant to open your heart, not to fixate your mind.

You must be compassionate. You must be tolerant. You must learn about others' understanding. You must see that the great faith is beyond religious belief alone.

You must take the Steps to Knowledge so that you may find the deeper voice that God has put within you to follow and to find. For it is only in this way that you can be re-united with your Source.

Heaven blesses those who can respond and calls all others to true recognition.

Let nothing divide the human family now. Let religion never be an article of war or a justification for conflict.

Human tendency towards strict ideology must be recognized and managed accordingly, or humanity will not have the strength, the courage or the unity to be successful in the times to come.

The Presence is with you. God is everywhere working through individuals at the level of Knowledge. This is religion in its purest and most eternal form.

CHAPTER 8

RELIGIOUS VIOLENCE

As revealed to
Marshall Vian Summers
on November 2, 2014
in Boulder, Colorado

Religious violence has been a plague upon humanity for centuries, exercised around the world, always present, periodically very extreme.

It is a problem because religion is being used by those forces, those groups and nations, seeking power and domination, using religion as a justification, as a cause, as a purpose.

But this cannot be, you see, for God initiated all the world's religions because God knows that not everyone can follow one teaching or one teacher.

Therefore, to punish the unbeliever is a crime against God. To denounce those who cannot respond to your religion represents a confusion and an arrogance and a crime against God.

God knows that not everyone can follow one teaching or one teacher, and that is why God at different critical times in human history has initiated new Teachings and sent Messengers from the Angelic Assembly into the world. Each adds something very important to the building of human civilization. Each is meant to be a counterbalance to others that become extreme and distorted in the hands of human leadership.

Religious violence now is tearing religions apart internally and is poised to strike others and one another at any moment. In a world of declining resources and violent weather and a changing world environment, the potential for religious violence is tremendous.

That is why God has spoken again, to call forth the truth about the world's religions—the truth of their Source, the truth of their purpose, what unites them and what requires them to understand one another.

God seeks to end separation between the world's religions, not to make them all the same, but to recognize that they are all components of a greater understanding.

But while God has initiated all the world's religions, they have all been changed by man over time—changed through adoption, changed through corruption, changed through misunderstanding and misuse, wedded with culture, used by governments to justify aggression and the subjugation of people. What is holy and sacred becomes profane.

Now in the world today, [the pure] religion stands as the one great thing that can unite people, but only if it is correctly understood, only if its Source is understood, its purpose, its meaning and its direction. Without this understanding, religion then becomes the ultimate justification for cruelty, violence and punishment.

Therefore, We must clarify certain things so that you understand very clearly the Will of Heaven, the intent of the Creator.

First, you must understand that all the great Messengers have come from the Angelic Assembly—half human, half holy they are, once they are in the world. Not ordinary people, but not gods either. The Jesus, the Buddha, the Muhammad, they come from the same Assembly, you see. So there can be no conflict between their Teachings if they are correctly understood and applied.

Next, you must understand that not everyone can follow the same teaching and teacher, no matter how gracious and wondrous they might be. God understands this, of course, but people are confused. That is why there could be no contention between the great traditions if they are correctly understood and practiced.

It is because God is wise, and humanity is foolish; because God understands the direction and the destiny of the human family, while people live for the moment and associate themselves with the past.

Next, you must understand that there can be no punishment, torture, cruelty or death in the name of religion. This is a violation of God's intent and Purpose. It is a crime against Heaven, you see. People are punished for other reasons, but [this is] justified in the name of God or religion. This is an abomination. There can be no exception to this. You cannot punish, torture or kill in the name of God.

Therefore, there is no holy war. There is no holy warrior. You go to war for other reasons—for power, for domination, for resources, for control, for revenge. It has nothing to do with religion.

For all true religion teaches tolerance and moderation. All true religion teaches humility and reverence. All true religion teaches compassion and forgiveness. All true religion teaches charity and service.

These are the most important components of religion, for this is what serves the human family. This is what keeps humanity from falling into ruin and despair. This is what elevates you beyond the animals and the creatures in the field.

To use religion for war, conquest and domination is an abomination. It is a crime against Heaven, you see.

Any scripture that promotes this is inauthentic. Any teaching that promotes this in the name of religion is inauthentic and incorrect. Any declaration, even from one of the Messengers, to promote this in the name of God and religion represents an error and a misunderstanding.

Think not that the Messengers were without error, for they all made mistakes along the way and had to be corrected.

To condemn people to Hell because they do not follow your ideology is an error and a crime against Heaven. To denounce people because they are unbelievers represents a misunderstanding.

If they cannot receive the Grace of God, then they are unfortunate and should be pitied, not punished. If they stray from their religion, they need assistance, not condemnation.

Who in the world can say what God wills for each person? The scriptures cannot contain that because God has been the Source of all the world's religions, so certainly the scriptures and the teaching must be for certain people only, and not for all.

It is human arrogance, human unforgiveness, human aggression, human stupidity and ignorance that give rise to the abuses of religion.

That is why in God's New Revelation for the world these corrections must be given with the greatest emphasis, for religion is being destroyed through corruption and misuse, through violence and subjugation. Its value, its purpose, its meaning, its Source are being lost with each passing day as religion is used by violent groups and people in the quest for power and revenge.

This requires a great correction, you see, or humanity will continue to fail and falter and decline, particularly facing a world of diminishing resources and a changing environment.

There must be great cooperation, great understanding, great compassion and forgiveness. But you see, these are the very things that each religion really promotes.

But the people who adopt religion must promote these things. It must be their emphasis. It must be their understanding. Or they will misuse their faith. They will use it to oppress others. They will use it to condemn their enemies. They will use it to divide and conquer other people. It will become cruel. It will become blind. It will become vicious and oppressive.

Such arrogance and ignorance are so apparent in the world today and have been demonstrated throughout human history, in every era, by every culture.

It is a failure, you see—a failure to understand, a failure to forgive, a failure to study and practice correctly, a failure to understand the will and the purpose and the meaning of God's Revelations, and why they were given, and why they all must be recognized in their pure form.

But their pure form has been lost to most people. They have become tools of the state. They have become the weapons of aggressive individuals and groups. They have become the sword. They have become the jail and the prison, and Hell and damnation itself.

You must understand that God's Plan is to save everyone and that the experience of Hell and Separation is temporary in time. Though it may seem long lasting, it is temporary in time.

For you have a holy origin and a holy destiny, and religion, if correctly understood and applied, will help you to remember and to recognize your deeper nature here. It will help you to come to terms with the fact that you were sent into the world to serve the human family, in specific ways, according to your nature and design here.

To worship God, to prostrate yourself in the mosque, the temple, or the church and fail to understand these things means that your worship is not correct. You cannot simply come to God seeking power and favors and dispensations. You are sent into the world to serve the world, using the true qualities of religion that We have specified here.

Without this, religion will fail in the world as it becomes more secular, more oppressed, more violent, facing great upheaval in the Great Waves of change to come. Religious groups will destroy themselves and everyone around them.

People will lose faith in God. They will lose heart. They will turn to technology to save them, thinking that it alone will be their salvation.

The Spirit and the Presence and the Power of God will be lost in a world of convulsive change and upheaval.

That is why God has spoken again, you see, to bring the Pure Revelation into the world, to teach you about religion at the level of Knowledge, the deeper Intelligence that God has put within all— waiting to be discovered, waiting to be followed, waiting to be expressed.

All the great religions are important, but they are all pathways to this Knowledge We speak of, you see. For this is where you unite with your Creator. It is not merely through belief or ideology or rigid spiritual practice and observance. It is by following that which God has put within you to follow, which is wholly pure—without condemnation, without grievance, without anger—without condemnation. It represents the part of you that has never left God and that is still connected to God and Creation even while you live in Separation in physical form in this world, in this reality.

To reunite with Knowledge is to reunite with your true nature. It is to finally become a whole person. It is to free yourself from the shackles of belief and ideology that oppresses and misdirects humanity at every turn.

The world needs this now because the world needs many to rise to serve, to prepare humanity for a future that will be very different from the past, to prepare humanity for its encounter with intelligent life in the universe, an encounter that is already taking place in the world today.

Many must be called, not only a saintly person here and there. Many must be called. But to be prepared for this means that your understanding of religion must be cleansed, must be clarified, must become whole, pure and authentic, or you will misuse everything We say here today. You will deny it or misuse it or try to wed it with your former beliefs, not understanding the real Message We are giving you here, which will save your life and the lives of those you love; which will restore your nations and protect them in the difficult times ahead.

This is the age of cooperation. There must be great cooperation, or humanity and human civilization can fail.

It is a great turning point that many have foreseen. It is not the end of times. It is not the end of the world. It is not the great Judgment Day that many people believe in. It is a great turning point for the human family, a turning point that will determine whether human freedom and sovereignty will be able to be maintained and built within this world, living as you are within a Greater Community of intelligent life in the universe.

The risks are tremendous. The calling for service is tremendous. Therefore, put down your weapons. Put down your angry rhetoric and condemnation. Put down your self-righteousness and your fundamentalist ideas, for they are nothing compared to the Grace and intention of God and what God has put within you to follow and to do. This represents the pure engagement with your Source.

For God is the Creator of countless races in the universe, and countless religions. It is not ideology or belief that brings you to your Source or enables you to cross that great threshold. It is service and alignment. It is the power and the love and the freedom to find and follow your way that God has given you, a greater gift than you can even imagine at this moment—greater than wealth, greater than having all your prayers answered. For only this will lead you out of the jungle of your confusion and your dire circumstances.

People of the world, hear Our words. We are the ones who spoke to the Jesus, the Buddha and the Muhammad. They have come from Us. And a New Messenger is in the world. And he has come from Us.

All the great Messengers of the past stand with him and support him, for they have had to endure witnessing their faith traditions distorted and corrupted and misused. They have had to witness human folly and religious violence undertaken in their name for centuries. You cannot imagine the suffering this has created for them.

So now they stand with God's New Messenger, praying that his Message can be received and understood, praying that their great traditions, which they have followed, can be cleansed and purified and made whole and wholesome again in the Spirit and Purpose of God.

God seeks to unite, not to destroy. It is forgiveness. It is compassion. It is tolerance. It is wisdom and restraint you must exercise now, facing the world you will have to face together.

People of the world, hear Our words. They represent your restoration, the return of dignity to you and purpose, meaning and value. They alone can cure the desire for conquest and revenge and heal the deep wounds of human abuse and corruption.

Understand that religion should never rule the nation, for this will corrupt religion completely. Religion is here to inspire, to advise and to direct, but not to rule, or it will lose all of its purity, its efficacy and its meaning.

Nations of the world, hear Our words. You know not the Will and Power of the Creator and what God wills for the human family, facing a future that you cannot yet see or recognize.

Do not claim there can be no further Messengers, for that is up to God and not up to you. Even the Angelic Assembly cannot say what God will do next, so do not claim that your teacher, your leader, your saint is the only one or the final one, for this represents confusion. It is not up for you to say these things. Even if it is in your scriptures, it is not up for anyone to ever say these things.

Heaven knows who will be sent, when they will be sent, how they will be sent and what their Message will be.

The great hope for humanity now is that God has spoken again. A great Revelation is in the world, larger than anything that has ever been given to the human family before. It is here now in its pure form.

You can even hear, for the first time in history, the Voice of Revelation that spoke to the great Messengers and that guided them through their difficult tasks and trials in the past.

This is not to replace the world's religions, but to unite them, to restore them and to bring them back into alignment with God's real purpose and intention for the world, so they all may play an important role in preparing humanity for the great challenge and the great change to come. They must be part of the solution, not part of the problem, you see.

Be humble. Be willing to reconsider your beliefs, your ideas and your admonitions. Be willing to reconsider. Be willing to repent. Be willing to listen and hear. Have the eyes to see and the ears to hear that God has given you and not have them be closed to protect your former assumptions, beliefs and investments.

Heaven will be watching to see who can respond. And with the Messenger in the world today, the former Messengers will be watching to see who amongst their followers and their religious communities can hear and can respond.

For God has spoken again. God has come at just the right time. God has come with the Pure Revelation.

CHAPTER 9

HEAVEN AND HELL

As revealed to
Marshall Vian Summers
on January 29, 2008
in Boulder, Colorado

It is a common theme in humanity's understanding of spirituality and religion that there is a higher truth, a greater realm, and that there is a lower realm, a realm of pain and suffering. For to be in physical reality is to experience this pain and suffering and to see its manifestations everywhere around you. Yet the memory of your Ancient Home, the reality of a greater and more complete existence, is still recalled, if only for fleeting moments.

So there is this dichotomy. These two realities seem to coexist within the individual, within you. There is clearly the evidence of suffering. There is clearly the emphasis on separation and one's uniqueness, on how one differentiates oneself from others and on how one becomes isolated in life.

Yet there is also this reoccurring experience or notion or recollection that there is a greater life within you and beyond you. The fact that this exists within you is not only a hope; it is not just a dream or a fantasy; it is more of a memory. It is a thread of reality that exists throughout your life in the physical universe—a thread that can be avoided and forgotten, but not extinguished.

The memory of it will come to you perhaps only fleetingly at times of great distress, at times of great comfort, at times when you are out of your ordinary state of mind. There is the sense that you are here for a purpose, that this life is not your ultimate reality, that you are passing through, that you are on a journey, that you have taken a sojourn into the physical reality to accomplish something, something that you have not yet discovered.

In a conceptual form, and in an extreme conceptual form, this begins the idea of Heaven and Hell. Heaven and Hell are kind of a use, or a manipulation, of this deeper awareness, the awareness of one's suffering and the awareness that one is connected to a greater life, somewhere, somehow.

The idea of Heaven that has been created in the world is a natural product of this awareness, but it has taken some extreme and some very distorted forms. In many religious teachings, Heaven is kind of a reward for doing well in life, for believing in God, for following God's edicts and the edicts of religion—a kind of future reward, a better life awaiting you, but a life that can only be achieved by meeting certain expectations and requirements.

Hell has been created as a place of punishment. For those who fail to meet these requirements and expectations, they go to a much worse place, a place even worse than their physical existence—a Hell which, in some traditions, has been described in detail.

So Heaven is the reward and Hell is a punishment. And yet God is often depicted as all merciful, all loving. So how can there be this notion of Hell if God is all merciful and all loving? And why would God be so upset with individuals when God knows exactly what they are going to do and when God understands that they are in a reality where error is so prevalent and the seductions of error are so great, there are very few people who could ever surmount them?

This [contradiction], of course, has led to a rejection of religion and, for some, a rejection of God altogether. Yet they cannot deny that they have a spiritual reality within themselves, something that does not seem to be the product of their culture or even of their physical existence.

Heaven has been depicted as a physical place where you are happy all the time, where there is no pain, no death and no suffering, but [where] you are still in some kind of physical form. When you think about it, to be in the physical form for eternity, with no contrasts in life, with nothing really to do with this body that you still have in this imagined Heaven, Heaven becomes extremely dull and boring. You cannot sing, "Glory Hallelujah" forever without becoming weary of it, of course.

So Heaven, though it seems a great reprieve from the difficulties of your current existence, seems to have no real relief on an ongoing basis. Given your current state of consciousness, given your identification with your body and your slavish response to the needs and the desires associated with the body, what would Heaven really look like if you were still in a physical state?

Everyone will get tired of praising God, and God does not need to be praised anyway, so the whole idea becomes rather silly after a while. If you are in Heaven and you still have a body, the body is still a problem—feeding it, housing it, keeping it comfortable. Then there is the need for change and the desire for things. Heaven certainly cannot be a great shopping spree. It cannot be a place of constant sensual pleasure without creating the kind of uncertainty and inner discord that such experiences create for people even here [on Earth].

So there are all these ideas of Heaven as a physical place where you have a kind of painless physical existence, and then, of course, there is a Hell which is a kind of punishment, where you did not make the grade, where you did not achieve the goal or you were not a good boy or a good girl in God's estimation.

Of course, some people look at all this and think it is madness and reject religion altogether, still holding on to some kind of notion that they have some kind of connection to a greater life or that they have a spiritual reality that is not merely a function of their psychology or physical needs in the world.

Here God becomes something you have to please, and when you have to please another, it breeds resentment and resistance, which makes error and personal indulgence, even destructive personal indulgence, have a kind of attraction. This attraction is associated with some kind of demonic figure who is always drawing you away from God.

This is prevalent in many of the world's religions—that there are loving spirits and evil spirits and there is kind of a tug of war going on between the pull of Heaven and the attractions of Hell. This is clearly borne out in a person's experience because there *is* a kind of tug of war within them.

The New Message from God that has been sent into the world brings clarity here if one seeks resolution. For the projection of Heaven and the projection of Hell all come from your current existence, whereas the reality of Heaven and the seeming reality of Hell are certainly beyond your current experience. So how can you project your ideas of what these things really are from your current position? They are imagined only.

You imagine Heaven to meet your current needs and expectations, and you fear Hell and you imagine Hell as a kind of further fall from grace, a worse condition. And, of course, these imagined Heavens and imagined Hells are used by institutions and traditions to try to corral people into good behavior, to try to even inspire good work, good citizenship or adherence to the religious principles or to the religious organization itself.

Clearly the real Heaven, and there is a real Heaven, is certainly beyond your estimation. And it is certainly beyond what your imagination can reveal to you. It is a different state altogether. And certainly if there is a Hell that is worse than your current condition, it too would be beyond your estimation. No matter how much you project your fears upon Hell and your desires upon Heaven, these two realities are beyond your current existence, and you cannot conceive of them. Nor can religious institutions create an accurate picture of what they really are, for they too are functioning out of your current reality, which is neither Heaven nor Hell.

The New Message from God then brings a clarity, but the clarity must be understood in the terms of existing at different levels. If you are at the bottom of the mountain, you cannot really imagine what it is like to be at the top unless you have spent a lot of time at very high elevations. And if you have only lived high up in the mountains, how can you imagine what it is to live an entirely different existence, down near the shore, down near the lowlands?

The New Message reveals that you have been sent into the world to serve a world in need, that you have come from an entirely different reality where who you are is known, where you are fully connected, where there are very few questions and the answer is ever present, into a reality where there are endless questions and very few answers, where you are alone and unknown to others and even to yourself.

You have had to take form, now having to take care of a body that has tremendous needs—a very fragile instrument that can be harmed, damaged or destroyed by any number of things. It has to be fed; it has to be clothed; it has to be protected. It is subject to illness and breakdown. It is something now that requires a tremendous amount of care and attention. And it seems to give you an identity in the world, a unique identity so that now your identity is explained in terms of your physical characteristics, the color of your skin, and beyond this the peculiarities of your individual personality and the consciousness that you have developed, that has been greatly conditioned by your family, your culture and your religion.

Here you become something entirely different from what you were before. You become an individual who is now identified with their body and with their ideas and with the ideas of their culture and the customs of their culture. And your culture tells you who you are and what you must do and how you must behave and what is expected of you and what you may be able to do to meet the needs of your body to survive, to be comfortable, to have your needs met. And, of course, there are very unique and different political situations and social customs to which you must adapt.

And so your life here becomes all consuming. Every minute of the day you are involved in adaptation, or the quest for resources, or the attempt to get along with others who are governed by their own incentives, who do not know you and who are unknown to you. And from this position you try to imagine Heaven, which is only a better version of what you are experiencing now.

But God has placed within you Knowledge, a deeper Mind—not a mind that questions, speculates, contrasts and condemns, but a Mind that is certain, a Mind that knows, a Mind that knows why you have come into the world, a Mind that is not deceived by all the terrors and seductions of your physical existence, a Mind that is free from your manipulation, a Mind that you carry like a secret cargo within you, a hidden treasure, a treasure at the very bottom and hold of the ship that you are trying to sail in the world.

And the memory of your Ancient Home, though seemingly blotted out by your current experience, is there nonetheless. It shines like the sun beyond the clouds. And though you live in a very cloudy world where this sun seems to barely shine through, it is there nonetheless.

You can identify yourself with any kind of group or political movement or religious association. You can consider yourself in any number of ways. There is a great number of characterizations to choose from here. You can identify yourself with your thoughts, your emotions, your tendencies, your addictions, your passions, your likes, your dislikes—everything that seems to make you appear to be unique—that which you suffer over, that which you desire. And yet there is this thread of truth within you that cannot be lost. It can be denied and forgotten, but it is still there.

There is a lifeline to your Ancient Home. It is kept alive by Knowledge within you. You can deny religion. You can deny God. You can claim that you are an animal only. You can create a very firm belief regarding these things. But Knowledge is still within you.

You can deny the existence of Knowledge. You can say it is all biochemistry. You can say it is all the hopes and dreams of a suffering animal who is aware of its own mortality and its own suffering. You can make any argument you want and claim great approval from others who are of like mind. But you cannot destroy Knowledge.

It just will remain silent within you until you come to your senses, until you have some kind of experience where you begin to realize that you are more than flesh and blood, that you are greater than your psychology and whatever current stream of thoughts are preoccupying you in the moment.

And though you may not have any notion of Heaven, you know you are connected to something greater beyond the physical realm, beyond your visual range. Beyond all the things that dominate your current awareness and existence, there is something greater beyond.

And you do not need to be religious to have this experience. You do not need to even have a religion. You can claim you are an atheist, and yet the Knowledge that God has placed within you is still there, waiting to be discovered. And its presence is something that you cannot completely shake off or deny. It is like a constant thread in your life.

You love yourself, you hate yourself. You go here, you go there. You go in and out of relationship with others. You change your circumstances; you change your philosophy. But there is something in you that does not change. It is there. It is like your heart keeps beating no matter what you are doing, no matter what you are thinking, no matter what you are believing; your heart is still beating. It is kind of like this except that Knowledge does not cease at the end of life.

And regarding Hell, you are living in a kind of Hell, the Hell of Separation. You are not sent into the world as a kind of punishment.

It is not a penal colony. It is not a place where people are sent because they were bad in Heaven. "Well, you were bad in Heaven, and now you have to go to Earth or to some other world in the Greater Community of worlds." You have chosen to come into this reality because part of Creation is existing within the physical reality, and you desire to come here to contribute and also to redeem yourself for anything that you have thought or done that is foreign, alien or destructive to your nature.

So there is the perfect Knowledge that you need to come here and your Spiritual Family, your learning group that God has assembled to assist you, that brings you here. You enter the world. You pass through a state of amnesia. You come into the world with senses open, impressionable, waiting to be imprinted by your family and your culture and your circumstances.

You have to have this state of amnesia because if you remembered your Ancient Home, you would simply not want to be here. You would want to turn around and go back immediately. When you came into the bright lights and chill of the world, you would just want to turn around and go back. So the amnesia is necessary to enable you to be here, to give you an incentive for being here, to give you a chance to be here. Otherwise, you go from a place of complete security and complete relationship to a place of complete insecurity and a place where relationships are very difficult to establish and maintain. You come from a place where you do not have a physical body, at least not in the firm form that you experience now, to a place where you have to take care of this physical vehicle in all of its many needs and problems.

So you pass through a state of amnesia. You come into the world. Here you are. And your identity begins to form from day one. You are given a name. Your body is identified as having certain characteristics, which are either desirable or undesirable to others. You are given roles and functions within your family. You are educated in your schools. If your culture is religious in its focus, you are given the teachings of religion. And by the time you are a young adult, well, you have been fully conditioned to fit in with whatever your culture expects of you.

But of course people do not fit in, and their real nature cannot be harnessed. It cannot be recreated completely. And so there is a wild part of you—a part that is beyond the dictates of family, culture and religion; a part that people fear and often try to indulge in, in destructive ways. That is because your true nature cannot be shaped to meet your current requirements and expectations completely. And that is because Knowledge lives within you, because Knowledge *is* your true nature, a nature created by God, a nature that is part of God, that is connected to God, that is responsive to God.

You can choose whether you want to be religious or spiritually oriented in the world, but you cannot choose the true nature that exists within you. You can choose to experience it or not, but you cannot choose whether it exists or not.

It is so fortunate for you that this is true. If you could really separate yourself from God, well, then Hell and tragedy would be forever real. But you cannot ultimately separate yourself from God. And so Hell must be temporary. Whatever manifestations Hell takes within your physical realm and beyond your physical realm, then it is temporary.

If you think you are in Hell because God is angry at you, well, that does not make any sense at all. Why would God be angry with you when God knows the mistakes you are going to make? When God has sent you into such a compromised situation, the likelihood of your committing serious mistakes is inevitable and overwhelming in an environment where real purity is so rare as to be beyond the reach and expectation of others.

You can claim that through grace, God can dissolve all error for those God chooses. But this does not make sense because *you* must choose. You must take this journey. You must fulfill your destiny here.

You could stay in Heaven and say, "Well, I'm just not going to go into physical reality. It's way too difficult. I've heard terrible things about it from those who have returned." But you know in your heart you want to come and extend your true nature here. It is natural to do that. God made you a giver. If you're not giving, if you're not extending, if you're not communicating, if you're not connecting, well, you are miserable, and this is, of course, what gives rise to the Separation to begin with and to Hell and all of its manifestations and imagined forms.

Of course, people try to imagine God as being a projection of themselves, just better and more powerful, but still given to anger and resentment and vengeance; still weak like themselves; still petty like themselves; still egotistical like themselves. They cannot imagine a God who does not have these things.

And they want their imagined God to punish others whom they themselves cannot stand, whom they see being unjustly treated or rewarded in the world. "Well, God will take care of *them*. They will be sent to Hell." They cannot imagine a God who does not send people to Hell. It is hard for them to see that it is they themselves who are in Hell and want to send others into a deeper Hell.

Where would religion in the world be today without a notion of Hell, a place of punishment? What would motivate good behavior in people? What would create social order? What would establish higher ethics if there were not a form of punishment, and that the source of this punishment should come from some God?

People seem to need to have the sword over their head to behave correctly because they are not connected to Knowledge, which would naturally guide them to think and act in constructive ways. Without Knowledge, they need some kind of overlord to threaten and to force them into good behavior. And they need to have rewards for their good behavior, rewards in this world and rewards beyond this world.

Now Hell, beyond your current existence, takes very, very cruel demonstrations—fiery pits and demons, torture and agony and all these kinds of things. And certainly there are worse and more contracted forms of Separation than what you currently experience. And indeed there are people walking around you that are in deeper states of Hell than you are.

And even beyond the physical, there are deeper states of Hell. Those represent states when someone leaves their physical vehicle, [but] they cannot return to their Spiritual Family because they have too much shame; they have too much hostility; they are too conflicted.

Some of these discarnate beings are still connected to the physical reality, haunting certain places, being stuck, being attached. Through grievance and shame and attachment, they cannot seem to let go of this place, even though they have lost their physical vehicle. They are stuck in a kind of limbo. But even this is temporary, for eventually Knowledge within them will free them, and they will find a way to work their way out of their predicament.

Then there are Hells of people who are in states of such self-condemnation that they are frozen in a kind of deeper reality. But even this reality is temporary, for eventually everyone will return to God.

But in time, this is tragic, for suffering is tragic. And suffering that is sustained is really tragic. But it is temporary. Eventually, the Separation will cease, Knowledge will emerge, and the individual will begin a path of reclamation under the direction of Knowledge, with the guidance and the assistance that God will make available.

There are, of course, people who will disagree with this because they will claim there must be Hell and there must be punishment and there must be justice. They think they know what justice is. They are the arbiters of justice. It is their notion of justice that they think that God must follow. "The wicked must be punished. The unrighteous must be denied Heaven. Those who have created terrible acts or who believe in terrible things must be punished," they think, and so they want God to do the punishment for them.

This just represents their conflicted state. This represents their own state of Separation. Lost now in the physical reality, they imagine what God is and what God will do and what God does to the wicked and to the non-believers. And so they themselves are part of the problem, you see. But God has placed Knowledge within them as well, and Knowledge is not deceived by these beliefs and these expectations, these demands and these admonitions.

Your return to God may be beyond human comprehension, but the Plan of God makes it inevitable. And God has placed Knowledge within you and everyone else to make the return inevitable. So the focus of your life now, then, is not to continue to reinforce beliefs in

Heavens and Hells. It is not to project upon God the role of the great punisher, the judge who sends those to prison and exonerates others. That is what *you* do, but that is not what God does.

God has sent you into a difficult situation and has placed Knowledge within you to enable you to serve that situation and to give you a way back. It is like entering a deep cave where the light of day is completely left behind, and you are in this labyrinth somewhere, and you are sent down there to help others who are lost in the labyrinth, and you yourself seem to be lost in the labyrinth, except that God has placed a little rope attached to you—an endless kind of rope that no matter how many turns you take, no matter how deep you get into that labyrinth, no matter how much you forget the light of day, well, there is still a lifeline to you. You may be lost, but you are not lost to God.

So the emphasis now is to build your relationship with Knowledge. It is to establish a connection with Knowledge, which represents your spiritual and eternal nature. If you do things that are wrong, well it is because you are violating your nature. And that is why you feel bad, and that is why you feel uncomfortable. And the more you violate your nature, the more it seems to recede within you, and you become out of relationship with your nature.

As is the case with your relationship with others, if you are out of relationship for too long, there is a kind of an approach avoidance. You are afraid now to reconnect. It is difficult. It is embarrassing. You become resistant to relationship, and this is reinforced by all kinds of notions about yourself and other people, but it is kind of a resistance that arises out of Separation.

This even happens with your true nature. You become resistant to experiencing it. You close your eyes for a few minutes and you feel the resistance. You want to be pulled back out into the world. You do not want to face what is inside of you. Perhaps you think it is all hellish and terrible, but really it is your true nature that is residing there beneath the turbulent surface of your mind. And now there is resistance; there is avoidance. And the Hell that you are living in still has its attractions, and you are identified with it, so to turn away from it is to turn away from its attractions and the identification. And there is resistance. There is anxiety. There is discomfort.

You must reconnect with Knowledge, you see. Your plans and goals, whether they bring you temporary pleasures or temporary wealth or a temporary sense of achievement, they do not meet the deeper need of your soul. They do not speak to the greater purpose that has brought you here. They do not resolve your fundamental conflict about who and what you are.

Through all the world religions, God has established pathways to return to Knowledge, but these pathways have become obscured by what religion has become and how religion is used. Only in the New Message, the pathway is reestablished without the weight of history, without the influence of culture, without the intrusion of human psychology. The pathway is clear. There is the pathway leading out of the labyrinth.

You love this labyrinth and you hate this labyrinth, all at once. It intrigues you, but it traps you and imprisons you. But you cannot escape it right away because you are here to give some things to the world, to connect with certain people for a certain purpose that only Knowledge knows. To fulfill your destiny here, these gifts must be given to the best of your ability. They will be conditioned by circumstances as to how, when and where they can be given, but they must be given, you see.

Otherwise, you will return to your Spiritual Family with your gifts unopened, your contribution not given, and then you will just want to come back because that is your desire and your destiny, you see. You want to come back, and you will say, "All right. This time I will not forget you. I will not forget Knowledge. I will not forget all of you who are sending me into the world. I will not forget God." But then you enter the world and you forget.

So the question becomes, "Will you remember?" And the only way you can remember is by reconnecting your thinking mind with the deeper Mind within you. Believing in saints and avatars, believing in redeemers, believing in what human religion establishes, that alone will not do it. These things can all be beneficial, but only if you are connected to Knowledge.

So there is great clarity here. The emphasis is clear. But the pathway is still mysterious, for you do not know what Knowledge is, or what Knowledge will guide you to do, or how it will express itself, or whether it will take you beyond your current parameters of culture and religion. You cannot control it. You cannot use it. You cannot manipulate it. You can only reconnect with it and follow it.

And, of course, there is so much fear about what people might do if they are guided by something within themselves, that this seems to be impossible or insane to those who have lost contact with Knowledge within themselves. They will be afraid of it. They will think it will lead to chaos. They think it will lead to the worst forms of human indulgence, human error, human folly and human destruction. And they think these things because they have forgotten. They are unaware that Knowledge is within them and that God has a Greater Plan than the plans they have for themselves.

So this does take faith, at the outset in particular, and at times of great self-doubt, and at times of great decision where you have to choose a way that you did not invent for yourself, it takes great faith, yes. But every step you take towards Knowledge, it becomes stronger in your experience. Your conscience becomes stronger. Your sense of what is really right becomes stronger.

This conscience is not established by religion and culture. It is established by God. When you violate your nature, you feel you have done something wrong, and you cannot escape this. When you do something that confirms your true nature, you feel good. You feel inspiration. It gives you a sense of renewal. It is like going hot and cold with yourself. You do something wrong, you feel cold. You do something good, you feel warm. If you want to go towards the warmth, you keep doing those things that give you a sense of warmth, even if they are very minor and insignificant. If you do something that violates your nature, you feel more and more distant and alienated from yourself.

So here it is not God you are trying to please. It is more about being true to your real nature, true to yourself, honest   honest at a much deeper level. Honest, not just in saying what you feel, but honest at the level of feeling what you truly know and having that become the basis of your communication and decision making and identification in the world. Your situation may look impossible, incomprehensible, but God has a way to get you out of the labyrinth, to get you out of this underworld of your own separated, personal experience.

To follow Knowledge, you do not have to belong to a religion, necessarily. It does not matter where you live, what country you live in, what your body looks like. It does not matter your social standing, your political circumstances. The pathway is the same. Though you will follow a way that is unique to you and to your needs and to your greater purpose, the pathway is the same.

Beliefs differ, interpretations differ, explanations differ, theological understandings differ, but the pathway is the same. If Jesus is your guide, it is still the pathway through Knowledge. If Muhammad is your guide, the pathway is still through Knowledge. If the Buddha is your guide, the pathway is still through Knowledge. The guide does not change the route you must follow.

People will disagree, people will argue, people will take issue, people will condemn, people will be upset, people will rage and be angry, but this represents their condition. This bespeaks their state of mind and awareness. Knowledge lives within you. How you regard it is determined by your condition, state of mind and awareness. But you cannot change Knowledge. And this ultimately represents your salvation.

The degree to which you are disassociated from Knowledge is the degree to which you are living in a kind of Hell. You could become more disassociated and live in a deeper kind of Hell. Your suffering could intensify. Your isolation could become deeper. Your sense of shame and guilt could become more overwhelming. But it is the same problem. You could go to the deepest part of the labyrinth and deny all possibility of redemption for yourself, but Knowledge is still within you. The Fire of Knowledge, though it may only be a little light, is still a burning ember within you.

After awhile, hiding and self-punishment lose their attraction, and Knowledge begins to pull you back to yourself, to your true Self, to your reality, to the reality that has sent you into the world. Even if you have committed the worst crimes imaginable, Knowledge is within you. It will have you make amends. It will have you do great works. It will give you great assignments so that you can experience your own redemption, but it is still within you, being the pull of God, the Presence of God and the Power of God in your life.

If you really want to please God, then praise and worship alone are not the way. You must really do what God sent you here to do. You must really honor what God has placed within you to honor, and you must honor this within others as well. And you must follow this to the best of your ability and allow it to express itself in a world of changing circumstances and difficult situations. This honors your relationship with God. This allows you to resonate with what God has put within you.

God does not need the praise, but God does need for the work to be done, for the gifts to be given, for you to experience redemption. God needs for you not to lose yourself in a world of terror, pleasure and disorientation. In the New Message, this becomes really clear. But you must let down your guard to experience this and to receive the great gift and to see that this is the essence of all the world's religions—religions that humanity has remade to fit its own compromised state, but which exists in a pure form nonetheless.

Think of Heaven as where you have come from and think of Hell as where you have been sent to serve—to help reclaim the separated, to support their reassociation with Knowledge within themselves and to create a world where Knowledge is more evident than it is today, where inspiration is more evident than it is today, where harmony and cooperation are more evident than they are today. It is like you have come from Heaven carrying a brick, and the brick is part of the foundation for a greater and more complete and more genuine reality here.

Everyone is here to fulfill their destiny in the world. The more they can know that and experience that, the world becomes less fearful, less conflicted, less divided and is more conducive to the true nature of all who dwell here.

CHAPTER 10

SIN, ERROR AND REDEMPTION

As revealed to
Marshall Vian Summers
on October 31, 2008
in Boulder, Colorado

The chief concern for people who are interested in religion is the problem of sin, the problem of human error, even grievous human error. And with sin is associated suffering and punishment. Even Hell has been created as a kind of ultimate punishment for ultimate sins.

While this is the foundation of much religious thinking, it is also the reason why millions of people turn away from religion altogether, even though they themselves are highly spiritual in their nature and orientation. Sin and punishment, then, becomes a very serious issue, and there are many theories regarding this.

God has sent a New Message into the world to bring clarification here because clarification is so greatly needed. God has inspired all the religions, but they have all been altered and changed by human misunderstanding, human ambition and human institutions so that, in some cases, what you have today is unrecognizable when compared with the original teaching and intention.

Clearly, there has to be an honest recognition of human error, its roots, its manifestations and how it can be corrected for the benefit of the individual and the benefit of humanity. God's New Message provides a very different understanding here, an understanding that is in keeping with the original intent of all the world's religions. Here sin or error, is associated with the individual's inability to experience and to express Knowledge, the deeper Intelligence that God has placed within each individual as a great potential.

It is as if you were born with two minds: a personal, social mind that has been conditioned by your culture and your family and the world; and a deeper Mind that is created by God—a Mind that does not think like your personal mind; a Mind that does not speculate, compare and contrast; a Mind that does not judge and condemn and project blame upon others. God has given Knowledge to each person to guide them, to protect them and to lead them to a greater life of meaning and fulfillment in service to the world.

This Mind, then, is meant to be the compass and the guide, the pilot to guide your ship through the narrow and dangerous waters of life. God knows that without Knowledge, with only your intellect and your social conditioning to guide you, you will be prone to many errors and many seductions. In fact, without Knowledge, most of your life will be prone to error. You will be constantly going off course, and you may go off course to such a great extent that it might not be possible within this life to bring you back.

That is why God does not punish the sinful because God knows without Knowledge all you can do is commit error—perhaps minor errors, socially acceptable errors, errors in keeping with the general beliefs and consensus of your culture, but errors nonetheless. These errors disassociate you from yourself; they disassociate you from others; they are prejudicial; they lead you to condemn whole nations of people whom you know nothing about; they lead you to establish extreme points of view, points of view that are cruel and oppressive when applied to nations and cultures. Without Knowledge, you will look through the lens of fear and desire, and you will not see the truth of your own nature or the truth of the nature of those around you.

Therefore, there is no punishment from God because God knows without Knowledge all you can do is commit error, even grievous error. Within Knowledge within you is a deeper conscience that knows what is right and what is wrong, a deeper conscience that restrains you from going against what is right, and motivates you to go with what is right.

This is not a social conscience. This is not a conscience that is established by the values and the customs of a culture. This is deeper and more natural. It is beyond cultural influences. It is fundamental to your nature.

Yet if you do not respond to this deeper conscience within yourself, if you are not aware of its existence, if you do not heed its warnings and respond to its motivations, then you will be guided by other things. You will be a slave to other forces—a slave to your own desires and addictions, a slave to the expectations of other people, a slave to your own fears and prejudices, a slave to the expectations of your culture, or to the admonitions and guidelines of your religion—a slave to so many other things. This is why people tend to be slavish, to think alike, to act alike, to act like sheep, mimicking one another, seeking approval from one another.

This is what people do when they are not guided by Knowledge. People abuse one another. They take advantage of one another. They seek to gain wealth and power, and to deny and even destroy others in their quests. They are seduced by beauty, wealth and charm.

These attractions have no influence over Knowledge within you, but to your personal mind, they are hypnotic. You will give away your life for them. You will deny life to others for them. In a myriad of different expressions, they will influence and capture you, and you will be bound to them as if they were your masters.

You will seek to acquire far more than you need. You will become obsessive in your acquisitions. You will spend whatever wealth you have lavishly, foolishly, on things of little or no value, while others starve and struggle to survive. As a consumer, you will be like a locust upon the world, devouring everything in sight, heedless and reckless, without regard for the human cost and without regard for the impact upon the natural world.

All of this happens because you are not responding to Knowledge. You are not being guided by Knowledge. God has given you Knowledge so that you would not fall prey to the seductions of the world and the tragedies of the world, so that your life would be strong, so that your life would hold true to your deeper nature and so that you would be able to fulfill the greater purpose that has sent you into the world.

Rich and poor alike, people are miserable because they are not fulfilling this greater purpose. For each person was given a unique purpose and set of accomplishments here, and if these are denied, either because of self-deception or because of the oppression of grinding poverty, then people will lack inspiration and integrity. They will either be forced by circumstances or by their own inclinations to be divorced and alienated from their deeper nature and from the Power and Presence of God within them.

This is the tragedy of humanity, and it is the tragedy of manifest life throughout the universe. It is the tragedy of Separation from God. But God has overcome Separation because God has placed Knowledge within you, a perfect guiding Intelligence—an Intelligence that cannot be corrupted by the world, an Intelligence that is not frightened by the horrors and cruelty of life here, an Intelligence that is committed to your purpose for being in the world, an Intelligence that cannot be dissuaded or undermined by any clever intention or dangerous force in the world.

So sin is living without Knowledge, and when people go against Knowledge, they create discomfort within themselves. If they persist in this, they will create a well of guilt, and guilt breeds hostility and blame upon others. And so the problem compounds itself until a person has no sense of value of other people and is driven by anger or resentment and need.

Here people can become truly destructive, beyond even what your cultures will allow. Here human beings are capable of incredible cruelty. This is an extreme form of being divorced from your deeper nature, from Knowledge within yourself.

People recognize, of course, the manifestations of crime and cruelty and seek punishment, and while it might be necessary in many cases to isolate an individual who is governed by these tendencies, people want more punishment. They want God to punish the wicked. They want the wicked to go to Hell and to be punished forever there. And they think that this is what God will do on the final Judgment Day. They think this because they think that God thinks like they do—with all of their grievances; with all of their prejudices; with their pride, their insecurity and their malice.

They do not realize that God has given them a Mind like God's—a deeper Mind, a Mind that has not been corrupted by the world. They think God's Mind is like their personal mind, just bigger and more powerful. Here the notions of a jealous God, an angry God, a vengeful God arise in people's imagination. That is because they are projecting upon God their own tendencies and their own predicament.

If God is all powerful, how could God be insecure? If God knows the mistakes you are going to make, why would God punish you for making them? If God knows that without Knowledge your mind would be confused and lost in the world, why would God punish you for this? That would be like punishing a baby for crying, or punishing a child for being childish. This is ignorant, and yet these ideas are very prevalent in the world, very prevalent among certain people in certain institutions who claim to represent the Divine will and purpose in the world.

People hope that the wicked who go unpunished in this life will find eternal punishment beyond this life, and that their sense of justice will be fulfilled, and their desire for revenge will be fulfilled, and that God will be their executioner, and that God will be their jailer. So the whole notion of Heaven and Hell here becomes a kind of psychological projection—a projection of human imagination, human values and human tendencies.

Clearly, Heaven is a state you cannot imagine, for Heaven is a state where you do not have physical form. You are not solid matter, the way you are at this moment, because to be in the body is to suffer the limitations of the body and the hazards of life. This could not be the heavenly state. Even if you had a body in the heavenly state, it would become increasingly confining and restrictive over time. And clearly, people's notions of Hell and damnation are not something that a loving God could ever create or sanction.

So you have these paradoxes and these conflicts and this confusion. It is all born of being disassociated from your deeper nature and from the deeper current of your life. Here imagination replaces recognition and comprehension. Here ideology and strict beliefs replace the certainty of Knowledge within yourself. Here your awareness of the Divine Presence becomes a kind of courtroom battle instead of the power of grace and redemption.

God knows that the physical existence is difficult and problematic and that within this, people will be frightened, terrified and driven by the circumstances of life. That is why God has placed Knowledge within you and within all sentient beings—as a source of guidance; as a source of correction, protection and inspiration. The problem of the Separation was cured instantly because Knowledge was placed within those who sought to escape from their heavenly state to create a different kind of reality for themselves.

You can imagine anything you want and anything you do not want, but Knowledge still lives within you. It operates within the realm of your five senses and beyond the realm of your five senses. It operates beyond the realm and the boundaries of your intellect. That is why it seems so mysterious. It represents your non-physical reality, and that is why it baffles your logic and your systems of thought. Imagination gives form to your thoughts and impulses, but Knowledge is beyond form. Yet Knowledge guides you in the most practical matters. God knows what is right and what is not right for you.

So Knowledge is the antidote to evil. It is the correction for sin, and it is entirely natural within you, being the essence of your true Self, the

Self that God has created, not the self that is a product of your culture and your worldly environment.

Before you make a mistake, there are signs, and there will be restraint within yourself. Before you commit a grievous or costly error, you will feel this restraint. Great opportunities will come into your life, important relationships, and Knowledge will motivate you towards them. But if you cannot feel this restraint and this motivation, then the Power and Grace of God are lost upon you temporarily.

Without them, you will only have your confusion, your ideas and the ideas of others to guide you. This is the source of all error. This is what produces costly and even fatal mistakes. This is what leads you down a dark road of error, guilt and self-repudiation.

But Knowledge is still with you, always with you. God comes along for the ride. The power of redemption is still within you. No matter what you have done, or think you have done, that you hold against yourself and others, Knowledge is there to provide the correction. It provides the way out of your dilemma. It restores your true relationship with yourself; it gives you the foundation and the criteria for establishing true relationships with others; and it sets you on the course to finding and fulfilling your greater mission and purpose for being in the world.

God has already given you the answer. But you must refocus your mind, and reorient yourself to experience the answer that lives and functions within you. This involves taking the Steps to Knowledge, reconnecting your personal surface mind with the deeper Mind of Knowledge within you.

You see, instead of punishing the wicked and sending them to Hell, God attends to the wicked, the sinful, and the ones who are lost and prepares them for Heaven by restoring to them their awareness of Knowledge, and with it their deeper conscience.

People often associate conscience with guilt, but really conscience is the awareness and the power within you that will lead you to restore your life, to erase your errors and to re-establish your integrity and your true relationship with yourself and others. It is the power of redemption within you. No matter how far afield you go, no matter how much you diverge from your true nature and purpose in the world, Knowledge is there to bring you back.

What about punishment? Well, when you divorce yourself from Knowledge, you are punishing yourself already. Giving your life to meaningless things, you will feel your life is meaningless. Giving your life to insignificant things, you will feel your life is insignificant. Being guided by desires, ambition and fear, you will think that that is what your life is composed of. It will be weak, fallible, and you will have no respect for yourself or others. And what you value in others will be those things that have seduced you: power, prestige, forcefulness, obedience and so forth.

This is a world without Knowledge. This is where the separated have come to live and to try to fulfill themselves here. But you cannot find fulfillment in this way. For without Knowledge, there is no fulfillment. There is temporary pleasure. Perhaps there are moments of being carefree, but life here is burdensome and difficult. It is stressful. Constantly having to problem solve and adapt to changing circumstances, life here is difficult. If you are being honest with yourself, you will see this and have to confess this. And you will compromise yourself to get what you want, to please others, to win favor, to build wealth, to capture beauty and to avoid pain.

It is a hopeless situation. You can think of a million different plans and schemes to work your existence to your advantage, but there is no hope here. The desire for personal fulfillment will not work because Separation does not work, and you cannot make it work, and the more you try, the more you deceive yourself and give yourself over to your ambitions and the ambitions of others.

People around you are demonstrating dramatically, and in countless ways, all the results of living without Knowledge. How can you condemn them for this, when this is showing you the value of Knowledge within yourself, and the hopelessness of trying to fulfill yourself without it? With a true understanding, there will be no condemnation. In God, there is no condemnation. There is only correction.

It is not as if you are a believer and you get to go to Heaven. That is not how this works at all. You must give your life to the power and presence of Knowledge, guided by your deeper conscience, whether you adhere to a religion or not.

It is not the believers that go to Heaven. It is those who are prepared for Heaven by the power and the grace of Knowledge within themselves. For this is what God has given to them to guide them and to prepare them and to fulfill them in this world, a world where fulfillment cannot be achieved in any other way.

Sin and error are the natural by-products of living in a state of Separation, of alienation from oneself and others. These are to be expected; these are the consequences. And whether these errors are socially acceptable or not, whether they are generally experienced and expressed by others or not, it is fundamentally the same problem. It is just a matter of how extreme one's involvement in servitude to ignorance and to Separation. But there is still the redeeming power of Knowledge.

Society must isolate those who are dangerous and destructive, but do not think there is eternal damnation. There is only Separation from God. And this produces a kind of continual discomfort and level of suffering that no amount of pleasure, escape or avoidance can allay.

So you are living in a kind of Hell already. When you realize this, and you realize that you cannot escape this Hell by seeking more pleasure, or gaining more security, or gaining more power and dominance over others, then you will realize that you must relinquish the reins to a greater power within yourself.

Here the intellect can begin to assume its rightful place as a vehicle of expression and creativity for the power and presence of Knowledge within yourself. Here you begin to exert the power of correction for yourself and for others. And you look upon the world with forgiveness because you realize without Knowledge, people can only live in confusion and will be prone to error and all the seductions of those forces of dissonance in life that prove to be undermining to the well-being and integrity of people everywhere.

You have come into the world to escape your heavenly state, but you have also come here with a greater purpose because God has come along for the ride. God is in the back seat. You are driving the car. You think you are alone in this car, but God is in the back seat. God is whispering in your ear—where to turn, where to go, what to do, what to avoid, who to be with, who not to be with. And as your mind begins to settle down, you hear this voice; you feel these impulses. This is God speaking to you.

You seem to be alone and isolated, separate from others, but God has come along for the ride because you could never really separate yourself from God. Even if you committed the worst crimes in this life, you still cannot be separated from God, and God will reclaim you eventually. But the longer this takes, the more suffering you will undergo, and the longer you will be in your own personal hell. You could create a greater hell for yourself, but still the lifeline to God is there.

Certain religious figures and institutions try to coerce people into believing in God and into being obedient to their doctrines and ideology by threatening eternal punishment and damnation. And they claim this comes from God, the Word of God: "Here it is in the book." They point to the book.

But they do not understand God; they do not understand the Power and Presence of God. They think it is a matter of belief and obedience, but belief is weak; it is of the mind. And obedience is slavish and shows no true respect unless it is natural and comes from the heart. You cannot be coerced into doing the right thing, for your heart will not be there. And this will only generate resistance and resentment and a misunderstanding and misuse of the great Revelations that God has sent into the world. In a sense, everything becomes corrupted here. God's great Revelations become corrupted because people use them for their own advantages, to fulfill their own ideas and tendencies.

Religion is meant to be a pathway to follow, a path of redemption and renewal. It is meant to bring people to Knowledge, to honor the power and presence of Knowledge within the individual. But religion becomes a tool of the intellect. Here is where fundamentalism arises and strict observance of the law, claiming it to be God's law. God has no laws. God only has guidance. God has given you Knowledge, so you do not need to be ruled by a foreign and distant power.

The Lord of the universe is not preoccupied with your daily affairs and does not control the events of your daily life. But you have been given Knowledge, the guiding light within yourself. And you have greater Teachers beyond the visible range who are there to assist you, to guide you and whose presence in your life will become ever more manifest as you learn to follow the power and the presence of Knowledge within yourself.

God has created the perfect antidote to evil and the perfect correction for error. God does not expect perfection of you here, only greater service to the well-being of others and to the well-being and preservation of the world.

When you come to see this, you will be so grateful. You will be so grateful that you have this guiding power within yourself. And you will be so grateful that there is no sword of punishment hanging over your head, and that there is a way out of your predicament, no matter how deep and complex it may seem.

God's New Revelation brings clarity here, clarity of purpose and clarity of meaning. It teaches the reality of your spiritual nature at the level of Knowledge. It goes beyond simple guidelines and admonitions to provide a greater inspiration and direction for you. It honors your unique design and your unique purpose and mission in life.

God's New Revelation is pure. It has not been corrupted by governments. It has not been seized by ambitious individuals. It has not been wedded to other things. It remains uncorrupted, unalloyed, pure and essential. But you cannot understand it fully with your intellect. You will have to experience it.

You will have to experience the power and the presence of Knowledge within yourself and acknowledge that you have a greater reality beyond the realm of the physical body, and that this reality is with you at this moment and every moment. You will have to understand that beneath the surface of your mind is a deeper Mind, and a deeper current of life and wisdom. You will have to learn to still your mind to feel the power and presence of Knowledge within yourself, and God has provided the preparation for this.

Never think that God's Revelations have already been given, for God is not finished speaking to the world. God knows that humanity is entering a time of great travail, where it will have to face the Great Waves of change that are coming to the world and the reality of life and competition from the universe around you. God has not finished speaking to the world, and a great clarification is being given and a preparation for a new set of events and circumstances, for which humanity is unaware and unprepared.

It is time for humanity now to learn what spirituality means within a Greater Community of intelligent life in the universe. Instead of being an isolated and tribal emphasis, it now must become more universal and complete. It is time for humanity to learn of its life and destiny within this Greater Community, and have a greater understanding of the real nature of human spirituality, and the power of redemption and renewal that lives within you at this moment, waiting to be discovered.

CHAPTER 11

THE MIRACLE

As revealed to
Marshall Vian Summers
on April 7, 2011
in Boulder, Colorado

Today We shall speak of the Miracle.

People have a very strange notion about miracles. They want to see fantastic demonstrations of supernatural powers. They hear stories of great teachers producing such events, and they are presented to them to induce or to strengthen belief—fantastic stories of producing miracles for people, as if that is what sets the true teacher apart from the ordinary person. This is the stuff of lore and fantasy certainly.

But what is a miracle really? We say the miracle is the discovery of the greater Intelligence that God has given to you and to each person and with this discovery the recognition that you are sent into the world for a greater purpose.

The miracle really is not just this moment of recognition, however. It is the entire discovery—for here you realize how God has saved you—and the promise of salvation for every person, no matter how sinful or evil they might appear to be.

The Mind of the Creator is so very different from what many religious teachings and principles have described—an angry, vengeful God; a judgmental God; a God sitting in Judgment Day, casting people into eternal damnation.

This surely must be the projections of the human mind—the human mind attempting to have God be the prosecutor and the executioner all at once—a projection of people's notion of what real justice is, projected now upon the Creator. Judgment and damnation are used to induce and fortify belief. People are threatened with the worst of consequences should they not submit in belief.

All this is projected upon a God that is expected to be all merciful, kind, loving and forgiving. So you see the great contradiction, and this contradiction is significant enough to turn many people away. This great contradiction, and all of the errors in thinking and understanding that are associated with it all represent the failure to recognize the miracle.

If you really understood how God is going to reach you, how you are going to serve God, and what is going to motivate and prompt this greater association and commitment, you would escape this conundrum, this contradiction, this absurd projection upon God of human values, human judgments and human expectations.

People who are not directly having a unique experience of the Divine are now threatened with damnation and torment if they will not believe. But belief is not really what is going to unite people with God. Belief is necessary as a substantiating and supporting emphasis, but it must support the true recognition, which in essence is the miracle itself.

The miracle is that you come to God on your own, recognizing a profound and deeper need within yourself that cannot be fulfilled by anything else: pleasure, wealth, beauty. Freedom, even, cannot fulfill the deeper need of the soul, for that is what brings you to God. And that is the miracle, you see.

THE MIRACLE

The miracle is that God has put Knowledge, a deeper Intelligence, within you. In fact, Knowledge is the part of you that has never left God. That is the miracle. And Separation has never really happened—that is the miracle. And you were sent into the world for a greater purpose—that is the miracle. And you can find and follow this purpose, and you were designed for it especially—that is the miracle!

There are extraterrestrial forces that can produce miracles as demonstrations of phenomenal and significant powers, using their technology and, in rare cases, even using the powers of their minds. They can fool you into thinking that they are godlike and that you should worship them, but is that the miracle? Or is that merely subterfuge and manipulation for the purpose of deception?

People want demonstrations of power because they feel powerless, because they have not yet found the real miracle in their lives, which restores to them their true power and efficacy in the world.

So there are the false miracles, the demonstrations that continue to impress and inspire, but these are used for unhealthy and unwholesome purposes. They are also used by the Intervention that is occurring today from races from beyond the world who seek to take advantage of a weak and superstitious humanity.

Understanding what the miracle really is sets the stage for true recognition of the Divine Presence, Purpose and Will in your life and in the whole world. The miracle is that God has planted salvation within you and that you can respond to this. In the end, that is more significant, more permanent, more marvelous than any demonstration of supernatural powers could ever be.

The fact that you bring yourself to God, based upon an honest recognition that there is a greater need within you that cannot be satisfied by anything else in the world, is part of that miracle. The discovery that God has given you a greater Intelligence, the power of Knowledge, to restore you, to protect you and to prepare you for a greater life in the world—this is part of the miracle!

You could say that your relationship with God is the miracle, for it demonstrates something that is so phenomenal and extraordinary and consequential that it can utterly change your life, restore you, give you greater power and integrity and reposition you in the world so that you may be of greater service where you are specifically needed.

The false miracles are only to induce belief, and belief is a kind of servitude. It is really not the genuine relationship. It is, in this case, a substitute for that relationship. You come to worship at the mosque, the temple or the church because you are expected to do so, because you want the rewards of doing so, because you are afraid if you do not do so, then misfortune will find you. But you have not yet experienced the miracle, or you would come to worship for a very different reason, and you would worship wherever you were—in your house, in your garden, at the city street, out in nature. You may not need a temple, or a temple may not be there for you.

Your purpose and your experience will be happening at a very different level than many people around you, who are going through the motions of religion, but they are not yet involved in the miracle of redemption. It is all belief and faith based—a kind of intellectual enterprise, a shallow enterprise, something that can fall away and is always eroding so you have to constantly reinforce it and revive it because it does not really have enough substance and strength within you to move you forward on its own, as if you were being towed along or corralled like a herd of sheep.

This whole notion has no understanding of the miracle, and your true relationship with the Creator, and your inherent responsibilities and purpose. Social forces, political forces, filial devotion—these become the prime motivators for people to believe. They want miracles from God because they feel so powerless, because they have not yet experienced the real miracle.

That God could guide you without interfering in your life, without manipulating your affairs, is a phenomenal thing that defies intellectual understanding. That God could allow you to exercise your fantasies, commit grave errors, even destroy your life and yet has planted the seed of redemption within you—that is something that the human intellect really cannot grasp. That you were chosen and are being called for something specifically that may or may not have anything to do with your local religion is something that the intellect has great difficulty comprehending. Try explaining this to other people, and they will look at you with blank faces.

The miracle is in you. It is waiting for you. It is calling you. It is waiting for you to come to your senses and to become honest enough with yourself to admit that you do not know what you are doing and that you are making mistakes and giving your life away to people and situations that have no promise whatsoever.

You return to God not because you are being corralled to do so, not because you are being bullied to do so, not because you are being threatened to do so, but because you are beginning to be really honest with yourself.

You do not return to your Ancient Home beyond this world because you are a firm believer because firm belief does not really establish an authentic relationship. Firm belief may be necessary as an adjunct to your original and authentic experience to uphold you during times of doubt or uncertainty. There faith has a real value. It serves its real purpose.

You return to your Ancient Home because you are rediscovering and expressing your relationship with the Divine, which defies and transcends religious orthodoxy because religious orthodoxy was created by people, but your relationship with God is created by God.

Here you may function within or without the boundaries of established religious institutions, but in essence your experience transcends what you can describe and explain. What Knowledge asks you to do and where it wants to take you is something that you must respond to—even if it defies social customs, even if it seems to contradict firm religious orthodoxy.

You know Jesus because you feel a relationship with Jesus, not because Jesus is producing miracles for you and you are simply there as a consumer, thinking you are getting something for nothing.

You know Muhammad because you are in relationship with Muhammad. You have a connection there that is intrinsic. It is part of your design and purpose.

The Buddha is inspiring to you because you have a relationship with this remarkable individual, not because this individual is making everything work out in life for you. In fact, your life may be a mess, a disaster, a set of immense problems, the consequences of many errors in thinking and judgment.

This is the difference between the believer and the person who is connected at a deeper level. Many people will go to God if they think they are going to get special favors, special dispensations or be rescued from their difficult circumstances. Oh, yes, the people will line up for the free lunch, for the miracle of the believer. But who amongst them is experiencing a real relationship here and comes to this relationship with their hands open, in a state of humility—without presumptions, without expectations of profit and gain, without running away from their life and circumstances?

God is not going to lift you above the world and make all of your problems go away. God is going to re-employ you here under the guidance of Knowledge. This is the miracle, you see. And if you can be redeemed, you do not just go back to Heaven. God employs you both in this world and eventually beyond this world in the universe as part of the Angelic Host—a junior part, at the outset, for there are many stages of development within this larger arena of life. It is not about going to Heaven [or] Hell. It is about fulfilling this stage of your preparation, or not.

You see, the reality is so very different from the general beliefs, assumptions and attitudes of people and religious institutions and so forth. That is why We bring God's New Revelation into the world, to clarify these things so that a more genuine relationship with the Divine can be comprehended and appreciated, approached and accepted. The illusions must be cast aside so that the reality can be revealed, established and fully experienced.

The miracle is not just one event. It is not simply that something wonderful happened in your life or that you were able to avoid difficult and painful experiences. It is the whole process of redemption that was set in motion when the Separation began—

before time, before this world existed, at the beginning of the physical universe, long ago.

God redeems the separated through Knowledge—in this world and in other worlds. This is an entirely new understanding for people. And with it, it requires a reconsideration of so many beliefs and assumptions.

The miracle of redemption can be found in every religion, but it has become so obscured and overlaid with other things that it may not be possible for the participant to really find it unless they have a very skillful and wise teacher to guide them. And such teachers are rare. You will find many who will reinforce belief and all that goes with it, but who will take you to the level of Knowledge, the deeper Intelligence within you?

For this is where God will speak to you and guide you. This is where the Will of the Creator flows through you, for that is where you are connected. It is like a current that runs through you at a deeper level, you see. It is not the same as your mind and intellect.

Your mind and intellect were created to navigate a difficult and problematic world and to learn to communicate effectively with others living in Separation. Your intellect is not who you are. It is not your reality.

When you leave this world, your intellect will fade away. To many people that looks like annihilation, but it is really liberation. Who you are now is free to expand and to express and to connect on a phenomenal level.

But right now, living in the world, you need the intellect. But you must understand that is not who you are. To gain freedom from your own mind, and the torments of your mind, and the restrictions of your mind, and the chaos of your mind is part of the miracle that God provides.

That which leads an individual to become a man or a woman of Knowledge is the miracle. Fully expressed it is worth more than a million believers to God.

God does not need praise. God does not need worship. God does not need all these things—great temples, prostration. That is for the benefit of the believer and the adherent. God is not insecure. God does not have to be bolstered and reminded how great God is. God does not need this.

You worship God to try to build a connection, to open yourself to the connection that already exists there. You prostrate yourself as an act of humility to say that God is greater than you and can guide you. But people do not understand the miracle, and so they do not see how this can be brought about. So they want dispensations. They want to be saved from their circumstances and the prospect of future loss and deprivation.

You may pray for these things, of course, and many people are facing grave circumstances, and they do pray for these things, and that is appropriate. But what delivers a response is at a deeper level, you see.

God did not create your intellect as it is today. When you started out in this life, your intellect was like a blank canvas. It was only a potential, like your physical body.

What your mind is today is a product of the world and its influence upon you and your reaction to it; and the decisions you have made and the beliefs you have assumed; the compromises you have made, your attitudes, your frustrations, your judgments, your unforgiveness, your fantasies, your desires, your fears—that is your intellect!

To free the mind from these things is a result of a revolution happening at a deeper level within you, and that is the miracle. It is a revolution created by God. That is the miracle. It is a process of transformation with many stages and steps. That is the miracle. You have been redeemed by a force you did not create. That is the miracle.

And now your mind is being dedicated to greater things. It is being focused on important things. And while old thoughts and fears may still haunt you from time to time as you proceed and progress, your mind has less and less of an impact upon your perception and experience, as if you had been freed from a prison house of your own creation and the creation of human society and human belief.

People who have not experienced the miracle will not understand it. They may even look at it fearfully, thinking that it could be evil, that they cannot trust it, [thinking] it should not be trusted: you should just believe and follow the prescriptions of religion. They will look upon the person experiencing the miracle with concern and uncertainty and even hostility, but they do not understand.

God has spoken to this person. Why not to them? There is jealousy. There is envy. There is misunderstanding. That is why the great saints and even the great Messengers who appear in the world every few centuries are maligned and misunderstood. Even God's Messengers are maligned and misunderstood by religious figures and by many people in the general population, but they do not understand.

They are fearful. They are envious. They want to be the chosen ones. They do not know what to make of this person who is having an inexplicable experience and doing strange and unpredictable things.

Governments do not want this. They want a compliant population that follows certain guidelines and principles without question. And so the person experiencing the miracle could be a source of concern to them.

You must know you are entering a world without Knowledge, a world that is guided by fear, desire and belief. This will help you to adapt and to learn the wisdom of not expressing your inner experience to the wrong people, learning to be discreet and discerning in this regard. For you want to nurture the miracle within yourself. You want it to grow. You want it to take you to the next step. You want it to become stronger and more profound and more continuous instead of just intermittent and periodic.

Therefore, the person responding to Knowledge must understand that they are responding to something very unique. They are experiencing a miracle, which is unlike everything else around them. They are experiencing something other people are not experiencing. Not yet. They have to keep the flame alive within themselves and be very careful who they share it with. Only someone else responding to the miracle can support them and understand them, or someone who has greater wisdom and is not governed by social convention and consensus.

God is calling you. That is the beginning of the miracle. Your response is part of the miracle. Taking the Steps to Knowledge is part of the miracle. Following Knowledge, letting other things in your mind begin to be set aside or to fall away naturally, if they are not really needed and are unnecessary for you, that is part of the miracle. Discovering a greater purpose and service in the world as a result of taking the Steps to Knowledge, that is part of the miracle.

Break free of conventional thinking. Allow your mind to respond to something remarkable beyond its comprehension. That is the miracle.

The true power and path of redemption must be restored to the human family—not just to one tribe or one nation, but to the whole world. And that is why We are bringing the Revelation of God to you. That is why you are being called.

Your desire for freedom is not only freedom from the aggravations and the hazards of life. It is to find the miracle, and to follow the miracle, and eventually to embody and to express the miracle.

Let this be your understanding.

CHAPTER 12

THE SPIRITUAL FAMILIES AND THE PLAN OF GOD

As revealed to
Marshall Vian Summers
on March 1, 2008
in Boulder, Colorado

Your presence in the world here is not an accident. You were sent here for a purpose. This purpose remains hidden within you, kept safe by the deeper Knowledge, the deeper Mind that God has placed within you.

This purpose is very specific. It is here to accomplish certain tasks with certain people, to serve the world both in your time and for the times to come. Its reality exists beyond your intellect and beyond intellectual speculation. It is a mystery for you to discover and to express.

This purpose is not reflected necessarily in your goals and ambitions or even your personal interests. They may reflect aspects of this deeper purpose, but they themselves cannot define it, for it exists beyond human invention. It exists beyond an individual's preference. It is not based upon desire or fear.

Should you follow Knowledge and be able to discover this greater purpose for yourself, your whole life will begin to make sense, and your deeper inclinations and the lessons you have had to learn in life will all now have a true context, and you will see the connection between them. This is entirely natural, but at the outset it will seem confounding and mysterious.

The world has so many distractions and seductions. It has so many difficulties and requirements that it is not expected that you alone would be able to discover this Knowledge for yourself or the greater purpose that it contains.

Great assistance is available to you—assistance both from within the world and from beyond. There are certain individuals who have come into the world to assist you, for that is their purpose, as it is your purpose to assist them. And there are those who will remain beyond the visible range of your life who are also here to assist you.

You live in a seeming state of Separation where you think you are an individual alone. But in reality you are part of something much greater. You are part of a Spiritual Family, a Family which must now raise you so that you can be prepared to discover and to express this greater purpose that has brought you into the world.

God knows that you cannot do this alone, that you will need great companionship, and you will need inspiration from beyond the world as well.

The God of the universe is not there to provide this to you personally. Instead, it is provided through a network of relationships, a network that exists already, a network that is so great and so far-reaching that you cannot comprehend it intellectually. But you can and indeed must experience it directly.

When people speak of experiencing the presence, a spiritual presence, what they are really referring to is the presence of their

THE SPIRITUAL FAMILIES AND THE
PLAN OF GOD

Spiritual Family—that specific group that is here to assist you in this great discovery, a group that has sent you into the world, a group that you are connected with intrinsically at a much deeper level.

While you may make lasting associations with people in the world, you may make contracts with them and bond with them, you may attach yourself to them out of desire or fear, you may even marry one or more of them, but the bond you have with your Spiritual Family is deeper and more pervasive. It is not built upon your experience of the world, for it was established before you came and will exist after you have departed this life.

Your Spiritual Family is one of the great teachings of the New Message from God and a revelation of what spirituality means within a larger panorama of intelligent life in the universe. For your Spiritual Family contains individuals who are not only human but represent other races as well. For God's Purpose is not simply to unite and uplift humanity, but to unite and uplift all intelligent life in the universe.

That is why it is incomprehensible to you. That is why it extends far beyond your current religions and religious understanding and religious teachings. For it represents God's Plan within the universe itself.

This is important for you to understand now because humanity is standing at the threshold of space, and it will have to contend with various forces from this Greater Community of intelligent life, both now and in the future.

This is beyond your current concerns and preoccupations, but it has everything to do with why you are here in the world, and where the world itself is headed, and the great challenges that humanity will have to face in the future—challenges beyond anything that humanity as a whole has ever had to contend with before.

To understand God's Work in the universe, it is necessary for you to consider the meaning and the reality of your Spiritual Family. If you were connected only to humankind, then God's Plan would not connect you with life in the universe. You would have no real intrinsic bond with life beyond this one world, which is like a pebble, a grain of sand, in a beach that extends beyond what you can see and know.

Redemption in the universe is not for humanity alone. It is not for this one tiny planet alone. It is not for one individual alone, most certainly. Again, this extends beyond your range of awareness and concern. But it has everything to do with who you are and why you are here.

Fundamentally, you were sent here to serve the times in which you live. Your service extends not only within the realm of your understanding and your particular activities and engagements with other people. It extends beyond this to support the evolution of humanity and to help prepare humanity for its emergence into a Greater Community of intelligent life.

You can see here how people's religious beliefs and understanding are so incomplete, how they are only a great guess and may only encompass a small part of their true purpose and value in the world.

God's Will is for humanity to emerge into this Greater Community of intelligent life as a free and sovereign race, independent of foreign manipulation and domination. This is not a problem perhaps that you have ever considered, or think to be important, or to which you would give priority concerning the other problems and issues that concern you today.

But it represents the destiny of humanity. For this freedom and this sovereignty and this independence will be difficult to establish and to defend in a universe where freedom is rare and where competition for resources is extensive and intense.

You see yourself in such a small light, and your understanding is so incomplete. But God understands this. It is to be expected.

You have come from a greater life to a far lesser existence here in the world, and in order to adapt to this existence in the world, you have lost much of your former awareness and capabilities. Much of this awareness and these capabilities must be established and regained if you are to comprehend your true nature, if you are to comprehend your greater work in the world and if you are to comprehend the movement of the world, if you are to comprehend human destiny.

The religions of the world cannot account for this fully, for they were given at a time when humanity had not yet reached this great threshold. They were given to establish a foundation, a moral and ethical foundation, for how to live in the world and how to promote human unity, human cooperation and human compassion. They laid the foundation for a greater human civilization beyond the sphere of one tribe or one group alone.

But they cannot prepare you for the great threshold of emerging into the Greater Community. And because they are currently so fractured and divided within themselves and between one another, it is very difficult for them now, given the weight of history and culture, to promote human freedom, unity and cooperation effectively.

You see, your life now is not simply in this one world. Your destiny is not simply in this one world. For humanity is emerging into a Greater Community of intelligent life. Contact has begun. But it is Contact with dangerous races who are here to intervene and to take advantage of a weak and divided humanity.

The vast majority of people are far too preoccupied with themselves, their current circumstances and their conflicts and contentions with one another to see the great challenge, to recognize the nature of this Intervention that is occurring in the world today.

Your Spiritual Family is with you. There are other individuals in the world who are looking for you, and you are looking for them because it is natural for you to do this. You have a great attraction to one another.

Do not think that every person to [whom] you are attracted or who impresses you is part of your Spiritual Family. Even the great weight of personal attraction cannot account for the deeper meaning and the pervasive nature of this connection with these certain individuals who are destined to be part of your mission and purpose in the world.

You have not yet the skill to recognize them or to discern them from the many other attractions that preoccupy you and that intrigue you. But as you become stronger with Knowledge, as you take the Steps to Knowledge to build a connection between your thinking worldly mind and your deeper spiritual Mind, the Mind that God has created in you, it will draw these individuals to you.

THE SPIRITUAL FAMILIES AND THE
PLAN OF GOD

Even if they are on the other side of the world, you two would try to find a way to one another. And there will be more than one, for this is not simply meant to be a marriage, a union between two people, but a greater association, though if you are married, it will be only to one person. Yet you have a greater association. This is your Spiritual Family. It is not simply a romance with one person.

Beyond the world, there will be those who will guide you and assist you—to support you in not losing yourself in your fears or your desires, and not giving your life away prematurely to situations and relationships that have no greater promise; to give you the strength, the courage, the patience and the forbearance that you will need to prepare yourself and to lay down a foundation for a greater life in a radically changing world.

Many people in many different traditions are encouraged to yield to God, to follow God, to follow what God has established, to follow the precepts of religion, to believe in ancient stories, to believe in the lives of the Messengers, the saints and the avatars. And, of course, people reject this or attempt it with varying degrees of fervor and commitment.

But the real nature of your spirituality is to be of service in the world, to bring something from your Ancient Home here, to support humanity's future, its evolution, its unity, its compassion and its care for the world itself.

You are not here because God hates you or has rejected you or that you are sinful. Your life is full of error, of course, because you are not yet connected to Knowledge. You have made many mistakes, of course, because you have not yet discovered Knowledge, which will prevent you from making these mistakes and will protect you and guide you in the future.

God knows this, of course, and does not condemn you for your errors. But it is essential that you gain contact with Knowledge within yourself, the deeper thread of truth of your life, the greater Intelligence that God has placed within you to guide you and to protect you and to lead you to your greater work in the world. This will bring into your experience and awareness the presence of your Spiritual Family, those beyond the world and those within the world.

Your life here is not simply to worship God or to please God. For God will only be pleased, really, if you can fulfill your mission here, if you can realize your greater service in the world, if you can bring your life into focus, harmony and order to free yourself to discover this greater work and to carry it forth, and to do this with as much compassion and wisdom as possible.

You do not need to be a religious person to do this. You do not even need to be part of a religion to do this, though that may be appropriate for you. It is not based on one's allegiance to a religious institution or teaching that establishes the meaning of your greater purpose here.

As We have said, this purpose will remain mysterious even if you have advanced in your experience and your expression of it. You may be a Christian. You may be a Buddhist. You may be a Muslim. You may be a Zoroastrian. You may be Hindu. Yet your greater purpose is beyond these definitions, for it is established by God and not by man, not by history, not by tradition alone. You may serve within these traditions or beyond them, but they themselves are not the defining issues.

THE SPIRITUAL FAMILIES AND THE
PLAN OF GOD

People, of course, do not understand this. They think that your religious commitments and views define who you are and even define your relationship with God—whether you will be saved or not, whether you will be redeemed or not, whether you will be favored in some end point or not. But this is a human invention. This is a human perspective. It is born out of human psychology, human needs, human fears, human desires and aspirations.

Your true purpose is created by God. It is not a human invention. It connects you with life in the world and life in the universe. For you do not know what redemption really is or how it can be accomplished or what it even means. You do not know what your Ancient Home represents. You just think it is a better version of what you are experiencing now, if you think of it at all.

There is the reality of God's Purpose and Creation, and then there are the limits of human understanding and human psychology. Never forget the difference here, for if you do, you will transgress your boundaries, and you will not see the nature of your own ignorance or presumption.

Maintaining this openness and this humility is important. It is essential in order for you to progress and to prevent you from becoming a force of dissonance in the world, a force that hurts other people, a force that actually works against the Will and the Plan of God.

Religion has been guilty of these transgressions throughout history, within every culture and within every religious tradition. It is the problem of the ignorant trying to assume the profound. It is the mistake and the error that people make in trying to determine God's Will, Purpose and Presence according to human values and expectations, according to the conflicts inherent within human psychology.

God understands this limitation, but many people do not. God understands your predicament and why, without the guiding presence of Knowledge within you, you could only make mistakes and could only come to false or incomplete conclusions.

That is why your Spiritual Family is with you. That is why you have a destiny with certain individuals who are in the world today. That is why there is a presence with you, for your Spiritual Family is with you.

That is why Teachers have been assigned to you, to help to guide you and direct you and to warn you if you are about to make a serious mistake. They do not control your life, but they are here to be a positive influence, a redeeming influence, an influence that gives you great reassurance, great strength and great confidence and helps you to avoid the calamitous mistakes that you would make without their presence and their influence.

When you are living in the world, you are always courting disaster. You are always at risk of giving your life away prematurely or entering into some kind of slavish arrangement through your work or your personal relationships. You are always subject to other people's influence, demands and expectations.

Your thoughts and your beliefs are established largely beyond your control by the passions, the assumptions and the demands of human society around you. Instead of being God's Creation, you become merely a product of your culture, its values and expectations and its religious influences and predispositions.

THE SPIRITUAL FAMILIES AND THE
PLAN OF GOD

This is what the world makes of you. This is how the world creates you into something so different and foreign from your true nature. This is how the world conditions your thoughts, your beliefs, your allegiances, your attitudes and your prejudices.

You think you think for yourself, but really you think according to what your culture has taught you to think. Even if you rebel against this, even if you are a rebel in your own culture and society, it is still determining your response. You think you are becoming free from it, but it is still governing you. Whether you agree with it or contend against it, it is still determining the engagement.

A rebel can be just as much a slave as one who adheres to their culture. It is not until your Knowledge begins to emerge within you that you truly can become free—free from the restraints, free from the beliefs, free from the overbearing weight of culture, family and even religion which turn you into something that is alien and foreign to who you are, that disassociate you from your deeper and truer inclinations and that commit you to people and situations that have nothing to do with your greater purpose for being in the world.

That is why your Spiritual Family is an influence and a presence. For without this influence and this presence, you would become merely a product of your culture. Whether you conform or rebel, you will still be a product of your culture. Your thinking will not be your own. Your values will not be your own. You will not even know your true nature. And true integrity will be beyond your reach, even if you value honesty and personal accomplishment.

Even if your government gives you freedoms, even if you are affluent, even if you have opportunities for personal advancement in your culture and nation, you are still a slave to other forces. You are a slave to your sexual urges. You are a slave to your financial needs. You are a slave needing the approval of others whom you think you need.

You are driven to marry before you are ready. You are driven to have children before you are really mature enough to assume this responsibility. You are driven into forms of work that cannot in any way support your greater service in the world. You are driven into groups and allegiances whose values are not your own. You are driven to commit your time and your resources and even your devotion to things that will not be a part of your greater purpose, should it ever arise in your awareness.

You are driven to assume beliefs in God that have little to do with God's real Presence, Purpose and activity in the world. You are driven to identify with your body, with your personality, with your traits, with your beliefs, with the peculiarities of your nature—all the while missing the greater experience of your true life and purpose and nature here.

Do not, then, underestimate the power of these forces in the world. If you can objectively look at others, you will see their immense impact. You will see their overarching influence. You will see how they condition and condemn people to lives of misery and servitude, and how even religion itself is used by governments as a weapon. Even the belief in God now becomes political and corrupted.

You either serve your social conditioning or you serve the greater purpose that God has placed within you. You either follow your social conditioning or you learn to follow Knowledge. For this is the power that God has placed within you to free you and to guide you and to prepare you for a greater life, which is your destiny here.

THE SPIRITUAL FAMILIES AND THE PLAN OF GOD

Your thoughts and your understanding, your passionate beliefs—these things must take a position behind Knowledge. Knowledge must guide you now, not your passionate beliefs or great assumptions or associations, if you are to be free to discover this greater purpose and to experience the presence of your Spiritual Family, who abide with you even at this moment.

You have the opportunity here to gain a greater understanding, a greater experience of the nature of your deeper spiritual reality and the Presence, the Purpose and the activity of God in the world.

God is not focused on this one world exclusively, but has set in motion a Great Attraction throughout the universe to redeem the separated everywhere in the countless races of beings who inhabit this Greater Community of intelligent life—a Plan so great, so profound, so expansive and inclusive that no individual could ever comprehend it. You are a part of this.

This is beyond belief. This is beyond assumption. But it is not beyond your experience, for it includes you intimately and appropriately.

If you can live with Mystery, if you can leave your life open, if you can respond to the power and presence of Knowledge that God has placed within you, if you can proceed without presumption, without needing to control everything around you, without needing to adhere to strict beliefs, then you can proceed. Then you can learn. Then you can yield to the greater power within you to which you must become faithful.

It is your teacher now. It is your guide now. It will show you the true meaning of life and your relationship with the Divine and who you are in this world, what you are here to do and how to recognize those who were sent into the world to assist you from all other forms of attraction. It will free you from the dominance of your conditioning and will give you eyes to see and ears to hear.

It is only with this greater awareness, this growing awareness, this humility, this openness, can you comprehend the life of a Jesus or a Muhammad or a Buddha or all the great saints and Messengers who have been sent into the world to keep Knowledge alive within the world, and to help and assist humanity in moving forward, to establish human civilization and to prepare humanity for its great future, both within the world and in the Greater Community itself.

There is a New Message from God in the world. It resonates with all the Messages that God has ever sent into the world. And yet it presents wisdom and insight and comprehension beyond what has ever been given to humanity before.

For you stand at the threshold of the Greater Community now. You cannot be foolish and divided in the face of this greater panorama of life if you have any hope of maintaining your freedom there. There are other forces intervening in the world who seek to gain control of the world and the world's peoples. For you live on a beautiful planet, a planet that is valued by others. You live in a world that is a gem in the universe, a world that you are despoiling and exploiting. And others seek to intervene to preserve this world and these resources for themselves.

You are the foolish stewards of a beautiful place. You must unite to protect it and to safeguard it and to learn to use it wisely or it will surely be lost. It will surely be lost to others.

THE SPIRITUAL FAMILIES AND THE
PLAN OF GOD

If you understand nature, you will understand what is being said here. Humanity could lose its pre-eminence in this world, could be displaced by others, could be enslaved and corralled by other forces.

This is, of course, beyond your range of concern and even your ideas, but this is the great threshold that humanity is approaching. It is this that the New Message from God reveals and warns you against to raise your awareness, to open your eyes to your true predicament in the world and the predicament of all of humanity and the great challenges and opportunities that lie ahead.

If you cannot respond to this prophecy, if you cannot see it, if you cannot even entertain it because of your preconceived ideas, because of the weight of your social and religious conditioning, then you will enter the future blind and unprepared, asserting your beliefs, asserting your national pride, but unaware of the greater forces in the world and the greater challenge to your freedom and to the freedom of all who dwell here.

Your Spiritual Family exists. It is there for you. It is a powerful influence if you can open yourself to it. It is part of a Greater Plan that humanity has not yet been able to comprehend. It is the Greater Plan that has brought all the world's religions here and initiated them. Even though they have been changed and altered and misused by people throughout history, their greater purpose represents a Greater Plan, a Plan that only a few in the world have been able to comprehend with any degree of real clarity.

If you are to serve God, you must stop pretending that you know God. You must stop pretending that you understand God's Presence, Purpose and activity in the world. You must have the humility to do this. You must have the honesty to do this. You must have the restraint to do this.

Once you think you know the truth, the truth escapes you. Once you believe that you know God's Will and Purpose in the world, you will stop listening to God's Will and Purpose in the world. Once you think you have the answer, you will stop asking the questions that must be asked. You will become blind and stupid and foolish and will lose your connection to the Divine. You will close the door to God's Wisdom and Guidance that flow both within you and beyond you.

Let this not happen. Let yourself not be a product of your culture. Let yourself not be a slave to the predominating forces in the world. Let yourself not fall into the trap and the ease of simply holding firm beliefs. Let yourself not be corralled and seduced by the demands and admonitions of others.

You have a greater allegiance in the world that transcends all of your human associations. You have a greater allegiance to God, who is not merely the God of this world, but the God of all life in the Greater Community in which you live, God of all life in the universe—a universe with innumerable and countless races of beings, so varied and so different from you.

To understand God now, even to have an approximation, you must consider God within this greater context, a God of the Greater Community, not a God of your history, not a God of your great stories and tragedies alone, but a God of all life in the universe, not a God that simply reflects your human ambitions and values and inclinations, but a God beyond them altogether.

THE SPIRITUAL FAMILIES AND THE
PLAN OF GOD

People want God to be like them, to be kind of a superperson—reflecting their values, their intelligence, their psychology and their needs, concerns, fears and aspirations. But how can a God of the entire universe meet these expectations? They ask God to be something other than God. They want God to be a fulfillment of human expectation. They want God to meet the criteria that human beings establish.

Clearly, this is false. Clearly, this cannot be. Clearly, you must come to understand this and to moderate your views, if necessary, to have the freedom to comprehend this and to consider it deeply for yourself.

This is not simply a human error, of course. It is an error that is made by races throughout the universe. It is the result of Separation. It is the result of living without Knowledge.

God has placed Knowledge in all sentient beings. Therefore, the calling of Knowledge and The Way of Knowledge are what religion means in a more universal sense. If you were to ask "What is religion in the universe?" what it is is The Way of Knowledge and the calling of Knowledge, for this is the calling of redemption that God has placed within all sentient life.

Regardless of the form that individuals have taken, or the appearance of their cultures or their physical environment, their physical appearance, or their individual or collective aspirations, this is the greater calling in all of sentient life.

This is the calling within you. It transcends belief and religion. It transcends human understanding. It transcends human history. And yet it dwells within you as a simple power, a great attraction, a great yearning of the soul.

So simple and clear it is, so uniform and so complete. It is not swayed by your fears or your desires. It does not make compromises. It is not something that you or any other person can manipulate for your own advantage. That is why it saves you. That is why it redeems you because it is beyond human invention and manipulation.

You can only follow it to know it. You can only carry out its direction to see its wisdom and its power. You can only learn restraint to hold yourself back from moving against it or away from it.

This is the meaning of your spiritual work and practice: to take the Steps to Knowledge. For only Knowledge knows why you are here, who you must meet and what you must accomplish. It is because Knowledge is the gift of God, a gift that you are only now beginning to discover.

CHAPTER 13

THE REDEEMER

As revealed to
Marshall Vian Summers
on January 18, 2010
in Boulder, Colorado

When you begin to look at your life honestly and to consider the wisdom of your past decisions and the quality of your current circumstances—in light of who you really are, in light of the fact that you have come here for a greater purpose—you will see that your life needs to be redeemed. It needs to be renewed and refreshed, given a greater purpose, a greater dimension, a greater strength and a greater integrity.

Most people who have escaped abject poverty are now running away from themselves, chasing dreams and fantasies, romance and personal goals. They do not want to have to face their real condition and the reality that they are strangers to themselves and know very little about their inner life—where they are, who they are and how they came to be in their current circumstances.

They are running ahead, trying to have this and do that and be this. They are running. The wealthier they are, the more they are induced into these mad pursuits, trying to lose themselves in their romances, in their hobbies, in their quest for wealth and power, in their accumulation of things, consuming ever more of them, for they are never satisfied.

Yet when you begin to really look at your life, perhaps following a time of grave disappointment or frustration, a moment of real sobriety and self-honesty, you will see that your life needs to be redeemed. Whether you live in splendor or in squalor, your life needs to be redeemed. It needs real purpose, meaning and direction. It needs to be given a real foundation—real substance, real value.

Many people realize this, of course, and they seek to be redeemed by others. They seek to have a redeemer, a great teacher, a great prophet to redeem them. They want God to redeem them, but they want it to be done through another person, and they want to worship this person and believe fervently in this person. They want this person to be perfect, immaculate, miraculous—producing miracles and phenomenal events. And this person that they have imagined, or created, they call "a redeemer."

They seek this in another because they do not realize that God has put the Redeemer within them, in a deeper Intelligence called Knowledge—an Intelligence that exists beyond the realm and the reach of the intellect, an Intelligence that is not corrupted or compromised by the world, an Intelligence that is not driven by fear, desire and compulsion. This Intelligence is so unlike the mind that you think with that your intellect can hardly imagine it. Yet it exists there within you.

People are not aware of the Redeemer within themselves. And so they seek to glorify an ancient person, a great individual, and they imbue that individual with all the qualities that they want that individual to have, not only to be a magnanimous person, but to literally be like a god on Earth—part of God, son of God, an extension of God, a God-person.

Having never realized the power and the presence that lives within them, having never been encouraged to search there and to seek the Redeemer there, they will now be led by political forces and religious institutions to glorify and sanctify an individual like no other, until that individual becomes like a deity, to be praised and worshipped. All blessings will be asked of this individual. And the belief will constantly be reinforced by the religious institutions that this individual is the God-person, the redeemer on Earth, perhaps even the redeemer for the universe. But how would they know anything about the universe?

There must be clarification here, or the errors in judgment and the manipulation of people's lives by institutions and by ignorant leaders will be so profound that the world will continue in its desperate course. It will continue to be dominated and destroyed through human ignorance, violence and prejudice. There must be a great clarification.

You cannot clarify this intellectually because your intellect cannot account for your origin or your destiny beyond this world, nor the Greater Reality that exists beyond the range of your senses, as limited as they are. Even your imagination cannot reach to the Creator of all life. Nor can you imagine an Intelligence, *the* Intelligence, that has been given to you and to all sentient beings—waiting to be discovered, waiting to be followed, waiting to be expressed in service to your peoples, in service to whatever world the individual resides within, within the Greater Community of life in the universe.

A great teacher points the way. A great prophet gives the warning. A Messenger from God provides something new for humanity. But none of them are redeemers. They cannot replace what God has placed within you to be the source and the center of your salvation.

People imagine that Heaven is going to a lovely place where you sing Hallelujah all day long, but nobody really wants to do that. People think Heaven is someplace where there is endless pleasure without pain, but you would find that tedious after a short time.

The point is that you cannot imagine the heavenly state. It is so very different from your life in the physical manifestation. You just cannot imagine it. You will only hope and believe it is far better than what you are experiencing now, and in that you are very correct.

God knows that not everyone can follow one teacher, no matter how great the teacher may be. In the universe, there are trillions and trillions of races. No one redeemer can speak to them all. No one religion could speak to them all, obviously.

The Creator of all life is more intelligent, you see, and places the Redeemer in the individual. It may take a great teacher to call the Redeemer out of the individual, to engage the individual with the power and the presence of Knowledge within themselves. And, indeed, this is the case. For rarely if ever can you find this power on your own, or understand its importance or how to follow it wisely and to express it without confusion or corruption.

Beyond the manifestations of religion is the Mystery, and the Mystery is everything. The Mystery brings the person back to their inner life, which, for the vast majority of people in the world, has never been cultivated or developed. They are like strangers to themselves. They only recognize the outward manifestations of their ideas and their behavior, but they have no idea where this is all emanating from, what it really means, and their deeper nature and their deeper purpose, which only Knowledge can contain.

THE REDEEMER

In this way, Jesus is not a redeemer. He is pointing to the redemption, to the power of the Holy Spirit, which is not a Spirit that visits people periodically. It is the power and presence that lives within everyone at this moment, waiting to be discovered.

This was his greatest contribution to humanity—this and the emphasis on God's Love for Creation—to repair and to replace the Old Testaments that spoke of an angry, vengeful God, who rewarded those who believed and punished those who did not.

Many people, of course, still believe in the old God, for that is the way they can express their anger, their vengeance and their prejudices against others. But God is not part of your psychological drama.

God has put the power of redemption within you, but it will take wise teachers and powerful relationships and courage and determination on your part to be able to take the Steps to Knowledge and to discover and to follow this power successfully. Just to be told that it resides within you will mean nothing if you cannot experience it, follow it and learn to express it over time.

You are still living in misery. Your life is unredeemed. Your life is unexamined. Your inner life remains to be discovered. You are wandering. You are lost, relying only on your beliefs and your admonitions to give you any sense of clarity, permanence or direction.

This is why Jesus will not return to the Earth, for his work is in the Greater Community now. You will have to follow his Teaching. You cannot drag on his coattails, pandering to him, questioning him, begging him, groveling before him. It was not his mission to put you into this point of position.

True religion is greatly misunderstood and remains greatly unknown, even to those who claim to be the followers of their religion. That is why God has sent a New Revelation into the world—to give humanity greater strength, greater promise and the true clarification of the Divine Presence, Power and Plan in this world and throughout the universe.

The Revelation will speak to the great truth that always has resided in all of God's great Messages for humanity. But it will present things that have never been presented in the world before about the deeper nature of human spirituality and about humanity's future and destiny within a Greater Community of life in the universe. It will speak of the Great Waves of change that are coming to the world that will alter the landscape of the world and the condition of humanity and the prospects for human civilization. This has never been presented before, for it was not needed before. But now it is needed.

If Jesus returned to the world, he would start a world war—the believers against the non-believers—and what would be the value of that? God has no preference over who believes in Jesus over those who do not. You are asking for destruction to want such an occurrence to take place. The wise know this. The ignorant do not recognize it.

Jesus pointed to the Redeemer. He spoke as if the Redeemer were speaking through him, guided and governed by Knowledge, sent into the world for this purpose—to be a representative and a demonstration of the Redeemer.

God does not have to try to micromanage your life, or manage a chaotic world full of ignorant, chaotic peoples in a universe of countless worlds full of ignorant and confused individuals. God has simply put the Redeemer in everyone, waiting to be discovered. This is because the Creator is intelligent and is not an idiot…a wise manager…the Creator.

So once the Separation began before time, the answer was given completely. And for you it resides within you, beneath the surface of your mind, in a deeper well of silence within yourself. There, if you can cultivate the ability to enter this silence and to be there in the spirit of reconciliation, humility and openness, you will begin to hear the Voice that speaks. It will speak in words or in images, thoughts, feelings or sensations, depending upon your individual make-up and orientation. That is the Redeemer.

Many people, of course, do not know of this. They are afraid of themselves. They are afraid they are full of evil and evil intentions and the devil is lurking within them at all moments. They want to believe in something on the outside to save them, for they think that they are imperiled on the inside, and full of sin and evil.

This is ignorance. Yes, you have ignorant tendencies. You even have some evil tendencies. But these are nothing compared to the power of Knowledge that God has placed within you as the Redeemer.

So there will have to be a complete reconsideration here, or humanity will continue in its ignorant and destructive ways, unable to respond to God's Messages and God's influence, which speaks through Knowledge in the individual. For throughout that part of Creation that has entered Separation from God, God speaks to the separated through Knowledge—not as individual messages, but as a Will, a Force, a Great Attraction.

As the universe physically expands, God is calling everyone back. God is calling everyone back not through death, but through service, through relationship, through fulfillment and accomplishment in physical life.

Your success in Heaven is based on your success on Earth. Therefore, God is all about success. But God defines what success means, how it can be achieved and what its expression really amounts to.

Here the greedy and the self-serving will be disappointed, for God has other plans for them. Here that which is greedy and aggressive within you will not find satisfaction, for God has other plans for you. Only the Redeemer can reveal this to you on an individual basis.

Here it is your personal revelation that you must prepare for. Without this, people are stupid and blind, believing the principles and the admonitions of aggressive leaders and ambitious individuals, cast now in conflict with one another, producing violence, cruelty and genocide in the name of religion, in the name of God.

Look at human history and you will know that humanity needs and must be redeemed. Look at your own personal history honestly and objectively. Does it really reflect a greater purpose and meaning in life? Does it reflect real integrity, real self-honesty and true compassion for others?

If you are truly honest, you will see the answer. You may be appalled for a time, but you must see this. It is not to lead you to self-retribution or self-denial, but to a true recognition of your greatest needs in life.

God is everywhere, influencing the separated through the power and presence of Knowledge—a greater Intelligence of which humanity knows so very little.

Religion, however, has been cast into idolization, idolatry. Religion has been cast into idolatry through fantasy and superstition, into magic and potions, degenerating through the levels of ignorance and the passions of humanity.

The answer is so very simple, but people cannot seem to find it. The truth is so very light, but who can bear it? Who can live it? Who can follow the power and the presence of Knowledge without self-deception, without manipulation, without confabulation, without trying to maneuver or manipulate the Presence to meet one's preferences and desires?

With Knowledge, you speak clearly. You think clearly. Your life has a pathway and a direction. And you are not seduced by beauty, wealth and charm. You see through the deceptions of others. You see the need and the plights of others. You look not with condemnation, but with compassion. For you know that it will take great effort for people to pull themselves out of degradation, not only physically on the outside, but internally on the inside.

People's minds are full of pollution, full of violence, full of degradation, full of hatred and mistrust. It is like living in a slum.

The rich may chase their dreams and dress themselves up, but inside they are living in poverty. They think God is going to reward them with all of their little pleasures and trinkets. But they are unknown to themselves, and they are afraid to stop their desperate pursuits. They are so afraid of losing now—losing wealth, losing beauty, losing charm, being disapproved of, being rejected by others. They are a slave to these things. Their wealth has only given them greater travail.

Instead of taking care of the poor, they are buying mansions for themselves. Do you think that represents the Will of God? In God's eyes, the rich are more pathetic than the poor, for they have squandered the gifts that life has given them, whereas the poor do not possess them at all.

Everything must now be used for a greater purpose—wealth, power, opportunity, resources, advantages—everything to serve the well-being of humanity. For you are now facing the Great Waves of change, which have the power to devastate human civilization. You are facing competition from the universe, [from those] who are here to take advantage of a weak and divided humanity, seeking to govern human perception without the use of force.

People know not of these things, but these are the things that will determine the fate and the future of every person in the world and their offspring, their children, their families. People are missing the great problems and the great challenges, preoccupied with things of far less significance, or often of no significance at all.

When you can see this even in a moment of real self-honesty, in a moment of deep evaluation, you will see the need for redemption. And you will see you cannot redeem yourself through your intellectual pride; through your technological achievements; through the exertion of power and aggression in the world; through wealth and splendor and the parade of all the other inducements and seductions that draw people into desperate and hopeless pursuits.

The Redeemer is with you. You may call the Redeemer Jesus. You may call the Redeemer Muhammad. You may call the Redeemer the Buddha. You may call the Redeemer Shiva. You may call the Redeemer any name that you think is significant, but the Redeemer has no name, has no personality, has no form. It is invisible and therefore pervasive. It can enter into any situation. It is not limited by what limits you in your physical reality.

If you misunderstand the meaning of the Redeemer, you will misunderstand the life of Jesus. You will misunderstand the life of Muhammad, and the Buddha, and the other great Messengers that have come to the Earth. You will misunderstand religion.

Everything now will be skewed and miscast. You will think of God as the great judge that rewards and punishes at the end. You will think all these things because your premises are wrong. You will miscalculate the consequences and the results of these premises. You will think God is terrible because you are terrible. Religion will become full of conundrums and contradictions that cannot be resolved because you do not understand the difference between the Spirit and the manifest life.

You think God is there to serve you. Even though you may not admit this to yourself, you really want God to do things for you. You want God to take care of your problems for you. You want God to erase your errors for you. You want God to make yourself feel better about your life. You want God to give you hope and promise. You want God to make Separation work so you as an individual can fulfill yourself in the manifest reality.

But God has other Plans for you. If you are too afraid of them, you will avoid this, trying to lose yourself in romance, hobbies, making money or just trying to resolve your problems in life. God has other plans for you. And that is the Redemption.

The power and the presence of Knowledge creates the Redemption and holds it for you. You cannot govern it. You cannot control it. You cannot use it to make money, or to find love, or to achieve your goals, or to fulfill your ambitions. When you think like that, you think that God is here to serve you. You may think God is blessing you, but you think of God as a servant, your little errand boy who is going to fulfill your desires because you believe in some religious doctrine.

God has other Plans for you. And God's Plans will redeem you and fulfill you; give you real relationships with others; allow you to experience grace and power and presence in your life; and lift from your mind hatred, judgment and aggravation.

Only God can cleanse your mind, but God does not do this like a magic trick. It is a process that you go through because you have to go through this process. You do not get redeemed, because God cannot undo what you have created because God did not create these things. You have to undo what you have created, with the Power and the Presence of God guiding you.

You cannot return to your heavenly state full of grievance and anger, fear and ambition. You would not even know you were there. You would not be able to function in that reality. It would be like Hell for you.

So your life must be given purpose, meaning and direction. Your mind must be uplifted and cleansed and placed into service to the Redeemer.

Here you must understand the Redeemer is one. You do not own the Redeemer. You cannot be in conflict with others if you are guided by the Redeemer and if they are guided by the Redeemer.

People can hardly imagine what this would look like or what it would mean because it is not a part of the life they have created for themselves. People still think they can create their reality because they do not know of the Reality that has created them. People are trying to be successful living in Separation, not realizing that there is no success there at all.

Your Separation now has been given a greater purpose—the power of redemption, the power of service and contribution to the world, the power of giving, the power of love, the power of self-discipline and self-restraint, the power of mental clarity and emotional honesty, the power of objectivity and the power of resonance with others. Only the Redeemer can bestow these powers upon you and clear and cleanse your mind so these powers can emerge naturally in your experience, in your life and in your circumstances.

Not everyone can believe in one teacher. That will never happen and has never happened. It never happens in any world in the universe. But everyone can respond to the Redeemer. In this, it is only a matter of time. Time here is measured in terms of suffering and misery. For the longer your life remains unredeemed, the longer you live in anger, confusion and disappointment.

Your pleasures are temporary and easily lost. You have no sense of self-awareness. You have no true direction in life. You are trying to seek pleasure, comfort and reprieve, but you cannot find these in any satisfying way.

It is because Separation has never really occurred, and you are still connected to God. The Redeemer is the part of you that is still connected to God, and that connection could never be broken.

You see, God is the Great Attraction. When you begin to feel this Attraction, it begins to change your life, incrementally at first. But things begin to fall away—old ideas, old preoccupations. Even old beliefs and assumptions begin to fade, and new things come to take their place as a natural transformation within you.

But you need a great Teaching. You need a great clarification. For the world is full of error and ignorance, and true religion has been misconstrued so thoroughly that people are led astray within it.

This is part of God's New Revelation. Do not think you can stand apart from God's New Message for humanity and understand it, for that is not possible. You must study it. You must experience it. You must see what it has to tell you. Only then will you understand its power, its potency and why it has been called into the world at this time, and why you have found it at this time.

You have a greater destiny to be in the world, but only the Redeemer within you knows what this is, how it can be achieved and the steps that you must take to discover this. To support this discovery, the Creator of all life has provided the Steps to Knowledge in a very simple form. Under the guidance of the Redeemer, these Steps are powerful and life changing.

But you must come to this recognizing the deeper needs of your life. You cannot come as a consumer or as a thief. You cannot come merely to reap the reward. You have to take the journey that the Steps require. This journey is individual to you, but its truth is held in common with everyone.

Give thanks to the Creator of all life that the Redeemer is close at hand.

Give thanks that no matter how difficult or depraved or unfortunate your circumstances might be, the Redeemer is close at hand.

Give thanks that God has other Plans for you and your life, for your plans can never fulfill you.

Give thanks that all will be redeemed in the end and that the caverns of Hell will be emptied through the Grace of the Redeemer.

Give thanks that the world is a place to experience redemption and to express its gifts to a struggling world and a struggling humanity.

Give thanks that you are in the world at this time to face the Great Waves of change so that your gifts may be called forth from you and that your life may be one of service and contribution.

Give thanks that you have a mind and a body to be vehicles for the Redeemer, to be vehicles for Knowledge.

And give thanks that you are part of Creation and have never been able to leave it completely, for this makes your redemption possible and inevitable.

Now it is a matter of time. Now it is a matter of honesty. Now it is a matter of self-awareness and coming to terms with the truth of your life.

The Redeemer is waiting for you and calling for you—calling you out of the shadows, calling you out of confusion and hopeless dilemmas, calling you out of the snares and the traps of the world, calling you out of hatred and judgment and all other malignancies of the mind.

The Redeemer waits for you, but time is of the essence. For this is your time. This is the time for redemption. It is a time of Revelation where God has sent a New Message into the world for the protection and advancement of humanity. This is your great opportunity. It will not always be there for you. For as you grow older, you become less able to respond to the Redeemer and to follow what the Redeemer is going to provide for you.

Give thanks that God can never be fooled by human ingenuity, human recklessness or human deception, and that a Plan so perfect has been set in motion that no one can destroy it. You can only avoid it or misconstrue it, misunderstand it and misapply it. But you cannot harm it.

Let your faith, then, be in the power and the presence of Knowledge, for this is the true Redeemer. This is what God has sent to go along with you everywhere you go in the world. It is speaking to you every day, but you cannot hear it yet because your mind is stuck up at the surface. You cannot feel it yet because your feelings are trapped in other things. You cannot respond because you do not yet have the inner strength or the self-confidence to do this.

In this, no one is a master, for there are no masters living in the world. Everyone is a student. Even the most advanced teacher is still a student—a student of the Redeemer.

Let this be your understanding.

IMPORTANT TERMS

The New Message from God reveals that our world stands at the greatest threshold in the history and evolution of humanity. At this threshold, God has spoken again, revealing the great change that is coming to the world and our destiny within the Greater Community of life beyond our world, for which we are unaware and unprepared.

Here the Revelation redefines certain familiar terms, but within a greater context and introduces other terms that are new to the human family. It is important to understand these terms when reading the texts of the New Message and hearing the Voice of Revelation.

GOD is revealed in the New Message as the Source and Creator of all life and of countless races in the universe. Here the Greater Reality of God is unveiled in the expanded context of life in this world and all life in the universe. This greater context redefines the meaning of our understanding of God and of God's Power and Presence in our lives. The New Message states that to understand what God is doing in our world, we must understand what God is doing in the entire universe. This is now being revealed for the first time through a New Message from God. In the New Message, God is not a divine entity, personage or a singular awareness, but instead a pervasive force and presence that permeates all life and is moving all life in the universe towards a state of unity. God speaks to the deepest part of each person through the power of Knowledge that lives within them.

THE SEPARATION is the ongoing state and condition of being separate from God. The Separation began when part of Creation willed to have the freedom to be apart from God, to live in a state of

Separation. As a result, God created our evolving world and the expanding universe as a place for the separated to live in countless forms and places. Before the Separation, all life was in a timeless state of pure union. It is to this original state of union with God that all those living in Separation are ultimately called to return—through relationship, service and the discovery of Knowledge. It is God's Mission in our world and throughout the universe to reclaim the separated through Knowledge, which is the part of each individual still connected to God.

KNOWLEDGE is the deeper spiritual Intelligence within each person, waiting to be discovered. Knowledge represents the eternal part of us that has never left God. The New Message speaks of Knowledge as the great hope for humanity, an inner power at the heart of each person that God's New Message is here to reveal and to call forth. This deeper spiritual Intelligence exists beyond our thinking mind and the boundaries of our intellect. It alone has the power to guide each of us to our higher purpose and destined relationships in life. The New Message teaches extensively about the reality and experience of Knowledge.

THE ANGELIC ASSEMBLY is the presence of God's Angels who have been assigned to watch over our world and the evolution of humanity. This Assembly is part of the hierarchy established by God to support the redemption and return of all those living in Separation in the physical reality. Every world where sentient life exists is watched over by an Angelic Assembly. The Assembly overseeing our world is now translating the Will of God for our time into human language and understanding, which is now being revealed through the New Message from God. The term Angelic Assembly is synonymous with the terms Angelic Presence and Angelic Host in the text of the New Message.

IMPORTANT TERMS

THE NEW MESSAGE FROM GOD is a communication from God to people of all nations and religions. It represents the next stage of God's progressive Revelation for the human family and comes in response to the great challenges and needs of humanity today. The New Message is over 9000 pages in length and is the largest Revelation ever given to the world, given now to a literate world of global communication and growing global awareness. The New Message is not an offshoot or reformation of any past tradition and is not given for one tribe, nation or group alone. It is God's New Message for the whole world, which is now facing Great Waves of environmental, social and political change and the new threshold of emerging into a Greater Community of intelligent life in the universe.

THE VOICE OF REVELATION is the united voice of the Angelic Assembly delivering God's Message through a Messenger sent into the world for this task. Here the Assembly speaks as one Voice, the many speaking as one. For the first time in history, you are able to hear the actual Voice of Revelation speaking through God's Messenger. It is this Voice that has spoken to all God's Messengers in the past. The Word and the Sound of the Voice of Revelation are in the world and are available for you to hear in their original audio form.

THE MESSENGER is the one chosen, prepared and sent into the world by the Angelic Assembly to receive the New Message from God. The Messenger for this time is Marshall Vian Summers. Marshall is a humble man with no position in the world who has undergone a long and difficult preparation to receive God's New Revelation and bring it to the world. He is charged with the great burden, blessing and responsibility of presenting this Revelation to a divided and conflicted world. He is the first of God's Messengers to reveal the reality of a Greater Community of intelligent life in the universe. The Messenger has been engaged in this process of Revelation since the year 1982.

THE PRESENCE refers to different but interconnected realities: the presence of Knowledge within the individual, the Presence of the Angelic Assembly that oversees the world or ultimately the Presence of God in the universe. The Presence of these three realities offers a life-changing experience of grace and relationship. All three are connected to the larger process of growth and redemption for us, for the world and for the universe at large. Together they represent the mystery and purpose of our lives, which the New Message reveals to us in the clearest possible terms. The New Revelation offers a modern pathway for experiencing the power of the Presence in your life.

STEPS TO KNOWLEDGE is an ancient book of spiritual practice now being given by God to the world for the first time. Steps provides the lessons and practices necessary for learning and living the New Message from God. In beginning the Steps, you embark on a journey of discovering Knowledge, the mysterious source of your inner power and authority, and with it the essential relationships you are destined to find. Its 365 daily "steps," or practices, lead you to a personal revelation about your life and destiny. In taking this greater journey, you can discover the power of Knowledge and your experience of profound inner knowing, which lead you to your higher purpose and calling in life.

THE GREATER COMMUNITY is the larger universe of intelligent life in which our world has always existed. This Greater Community encompasses all worlds in the universe where sentient life exists, in all states of evolution and development. The New Message reveals that humanity is in an early and adolescent phase of its development and that the time has now come for humanity's emergence into the Greater Community. It is here, standing at the threshold of space, that humanity discovers that it is not alone in the universe, or even within its own world.

THE GREATER COMMUNITY WAY OF KNOWLEDGE is a timeless tradition representing God's work in the universe to reclaim the separated in all worlds through the power of Knowledge that is inherent in all intelligent life. To understand what God is doing in our world, we must begin to understand what God is doing in the entire universe. For the first time in history, The Greater Community Way of Knowledge is being presented to the world through a New Message from God. The New Message opens the portal to this timeless work of God underway throughout the universe in which we live. We stand at the threshold of emerging into this Greater Community and must now have access to The Greater Community Way of Knowledge in order to understand our destiny as a race and successfully navigate the challenges of interacting with life in the universe.

THE INTERVENTION is a dangerous form of contact underway by certain races from the Greater Community who are here to take advantage of a weak and divided humanity. This is occurring at a time when the human family is entering a period of increasing breakdown and disorder, in the face of the Great Waves of change. The Intervention presents itself as a benign and redeeming force while in reality its ultimate goal is to undermine human freedom and self-determination and take control of the world and its resources. The New Message reveals that the Intervention seeks to secretly establish its influence here in the minds and hearts of people at a time of growing confusion, conflict and vulnerability. God is calling us, as the native peoples of this world, to oppose this Intervention, to alert and educate others and to put forth our own rules of engagement as an emerging race. Our response to the Intervention and the Greater Community at large is the one thing that can unite a fractured and divided human family at a time of the greatest need and consequence for our race.

THE GREAT WAVES OF CHANGE are a set of powerful environmental, economic and social forces now converging in the world. The Great Waves are the result of humanity's misuse and overuse of the world, its resources and its environment. The Great Waves have the power to drastically alter the face of the world— producing economic instability, runaway climate change, violent weather and the loss of arable land and freshwater, threatening to produce a world condition of great difficulty and human suffering. The Great Waves are not an end times or apocalyptic event, but instead a challenging period of transition to a new world reality. The New Message reveals what is coming for the world and provides a preparation to enable us to navigate a radically changing world. God is calling for human unity and cooperation born now out of sheer necessity for the preservation and protection of human civilization. Together with the Intervention, the Great Waves represents one of the two great threats facing humanity and a major reason why God has spoken again.

HIGHER PURPOSE refers to the specific contribution each person was sent into the world to make and the unique relationships that will enable the fulfillment of this purpose. Knowledge within the individual holds their higher purpose and destiny for them, which cannot be ascertained by the intellect alone. These must be discovered, followed and expressed in service to others to be fully realized. The world needs the demonstration of this higher purpose from many more people as never before.

IMPORTANT TERMS

SPIRITUAL FAMILY refers to the small working groups formed after the Separation to enable all individuals to work towards greater states of union and relationship, undertaking this over a long span of time, culminating in their final return to God. Your Spiritual Family represents the relationships you have reclaimed through Knowledge during your long journey through Separation. Some members of your Spiritual Family are in the world and some are beyond the world. The Spiritual Families are a part of the mysterious Plan of God to free and reunite all those living in Separation.

ANCIENT HOME refers to the reality of life and the state of awareness and relationship you had before entering the world, and to which you will return after your life in the world. Your Ancient Home is a timeless state of connection and relationship with your Spiritual Family, The Assembly and God.

THE STORY OF THE MESSENGER

Marshall Vian Summers is the Messenger for the New Message from God. For over three decades he has been the recipient of a Divine Revelation given to prepare humanity for the great environmental, social and economic changes that are coming to the world and for humanity's contact with intelligent life in the universe.

In 1982, at the age of 33, Marshall Vian Summers was called into the deserts of the American Southwest where he had a direct encounter with the Angelic Presence, who had been guiding and preparing him for his future role and calling. This encounter forever altered the course of his life and initiated him into a deeper relationship with the Angelic Assembly, requiring that he surrender his life to God. This began the long, mysterious process of receiving God's New Message for humanity.

Following this mysterious initiation, he received the first revelations of the New Message from God. Over the decades since, a vast Revelation for humanity has unfolded, at times slowly and at times in great torrents. During these long years, he had to proceed with the support of only a few individuals, not knowing what this growing Revelation would mean and where it would ultimately lead.

The Messenger has walked a long and difficult road to receive and present the largest Revelation ever given to the human family. Still today the Voice of Revelation continues to speak through him as he faces the great challenge of bringing God's New Revelation to a troubled and conflicted world.

———— ⌒ ————

Read more about the life and story of the Messenger
Marshall Vian Summers:
www.newmessage.org/story-of-marshall-vian-summers

Read and hear the original revelation *The Story of the Messenger:*
www.newmessage.org/story-of-the-messenger

Hear and watch the world teachings of the Messenger:
www.newmessage.org/messenger

The Voice of Revelation

For the first time in history, you can hear the Voice of Revelation, such a Voice as spoke to the prophets and Messengers of the past and is now speaking again through a new Messenger who is in the world today.

The Voice of Revelation is not the voice of one individual, but that of the entire Angelic Assembly speaking together, all as one. Here God communicates beyond words to the Angelic Assembly, who then translate God's Message into human words and language that we can comprehend.

The revelations of this book were originally spoken in this manner by the Voice of Revelation through the Messenger Marshall Vian Summers. This process of Divine Revelation has occurred since 1982. The Revelation continues to this day.

———————⟃⟃———————

Hear the original audio recordings of the
Voice of Revelation, which is the Source of the text contained
in this book and throughout the New Message:
www.newmessage.org/experience

Learn more about the Voice of Revelation,
what it is and how it speaks through the Messenger:
www.newmessage.org/voiceofrevelation

About The Society for the New Message from God

Founded in 1992 by Marshall Vian Summers, The Society for the New Message from God is an independent religious 501(c)(3) non-profit organization that is primarily supported by readers and students of the New Message, receiving no sponsorship or revenue from any government or religious organization.

The Society's mission is to bring the New Message from God to people everywhere so that humanity can find its common ground, preserve the Earth, protect human freedom and advance human civilization as we stand at the threshold of great change and a universe full of intelligent life.

Marshall Vian Summers and The Society have been given the immense responsibility of bringing the New Message into the world. The members of The Society are a small group of dedicated individuals who have committed themselves to fulfill this mission. For them, it is both a burden and a great blessing to give themselves wholeheartedly in this great service to humanity.

The Society for the New Message

Contact us:

P.O. Box 1724 Boulder, CO 80306-1724
(303) 938-8401 (800) 938-3891
011 303 938 84 01 (International)
(303) 938-1214 (fax)
society@newmessage.org
www.newmessage.org
www.marshallsummers.com
www.alliesofhumanity.org
www.newknowledgelibrary.org

Connect with us:

www.youtube.com/thenewmessagefromgod
www.facebook.com/newmessagefromgod
www.facebook.com/marshallsummers
www.twitter.com/godsnewmessage

Donate to support The Society and join a community of givers who are helping bring the New Message to the world:
www.newmessage.org/donate

About the Worldwide Community of the New Message from God

The New Message from God is being studied and practiced by people around the world. Representing more than 90 countries and studying the New Message in over 30 languages, a worldwide community of students has formed to both receive the New Message and support the Messenger in bringing God's New Message to the world.

The New Message has the power to awaken the sleeping brilliance in people everywhere and bring new inspiration and wisdom into the lives of people from all nations and faith traditions.

Learn more about the worldwide community of people who are learning and living the New Message and taking the Steps to Knowledge in their lives.

Read and hear the original Revelation *The Worldwide Community of God's New Message:*
www.newmessage.org/theworldwidecommunity

Join the free Worldwide Community site where you can meet other students and engage with the Messenger:
www.community.newmessage.org

Learn more about the educational opportunities available in the Worldwide Community:

Community Site - www.community.newmessage.org/
New Message Free School - www.community.newmessage.org/school
Live Internet Broadcasts and International Events -
www.newmessage.org/events

Encampment - www.newmessage.org/encampment
Online Library of Text and Audio -
www.newmessage.org/experience

BOOKS OF THE NEW MESSAGE FROM GOD

God Has Spoken Again

The One God

The New Messenger

The Greater Community

The Journey to a New Life

The Power of Knowledge

The New World

Steps to Knowledge

Greater Community Spirituality

The Great Waves of Change

Life in the Universe

Wisdom from the Greater Community I & II

Secrets of Heaven

Relationships & Higher Purpose

Living The Way of Knowledge

CPSIA information can be obtained
at www.ICGtesting.com
Printed in the USA
BVHW030753311219
568240BV00001B/33/P